"In this illuminating and original stu[dy] [...] limitations of 'worldview' as a fram[...] [...] [...] Christian education. He argues that the biblical concept of 'wisdom' provides a richer way of thinking about the difficult, imperfect, communal activity of faithfully apprehending reality in the light of Christ. This is a paradigm-shifting book on the nature of Christian education—by far the best thing I've read on the topic."

BEN MYERS,
Alphacrucis University College, Sydney

"For quite some time, a common view as to the task of Christian education is that, with a Christian worldview in mind, teachers and students are to interpret the subject of their discipline in the light of that worldview. Simon Kennedy argues for the opposite understanding. Rather than beginning with a Christian worldview, the task of Christian education is to achieve a Christian worldview. To this he adds the important point that achieving a Christian worldview requires not just knowledge but wisdom. While deeply immersed in the literature, this book is a fresh, imaginative approach, breaking new ground and compellingly argued."

NICHOLAS WOLTERSTORFF,
Noah Porter Professor Emeritus of Philosophical Theology, Yale University;
Senior Research Scholar, Institute for Advanced Studies in Culture,
University of Virginia

Against Worldview

Reimagining Christian Formation
as Growth in Wisdom

Against Worldview

Reimagining Christian Formation
as Growth in Wisdom

SIMON P. KENNEDY

LEXHAM PRESS

Against Worldview: Reimagining Christian Formation as Growth in Wisdom

Copyright 2024 Simon P. Kennedy

Lexham Press, 1313 Commercial St., Bellingham, WA 98225
LexhamPress.com

Print ISBN 9781683597810
Digital ISBN 9781683597803
Library of Congress Control Number 2024939334

Lexham Editorial: Elliot Ritzema, John Barach, Mandi Newell
Cover Design: Jim LePage
Typesetting: Abigail Stocker

23 24 25 26 27 28 29 / US / 12 11 10 9 8 7 6 5 4 3 2 1

For Hayley

Contents

Contents

Abbreviations

CW   Herman Bavinck, *Christian Worldview*, trans. Nathaniel Gray Sutanto, James Eglinton, and Cory C. Brock (Wheaton, IL: Crossway, 2019).

PoR   Herman Bavinck, *Philosophy of Revelation: A New Annotated Edition*, trans. Cory Brock and Nathaniel Gray Sutanto (Peabody, MA: Hendrickson, 2018).

PW   J. H. Bavinck, *Personality and Worldview*, trans. and ed. James Eglinton (Wheaton, IL: Crossway, 2023).

RD   Herman Bavinck, *Reformed Dogmatics*, ed. John Bolt, trans. John Vriend. Volume 1: *Prolegomena* (Grand Rapids: Baker Academic, 2003); Volume 2: *God and Creation* (Grand Rapids: Baker Academic, 2004); Volume 3: *Sin and Salvation in Christ* (Grand Rapids: Baker Academic, 2006); Volume 4: *Holy Spirit, Church, and New Creation* (Grand Rapids: Baker Academic, 2008).

He will not let your foot be moved; he who keeps you will not slumber.
Behold, he who keeps Israel will neither slumber nor sleep.

Psalm 121:3–4

O LORD, who for our sake didst fast forty days and forty nights;
Give us grace to use such abstinence, that, our flesh being subdued to
the Spirit, we may ever obey thy godly motions in righteousness,
and true holiness, to thy honor and glory, who livest and reignest with
the Father and the Holy Ghost, one God, world without end. Amen.

The Collect, First Sunday in Lent, Book of Common Prayer

Chapter 1

Can Worldview Work?

Christian education institutions, publishing houses, churches, and parachurch ministries frequently use the term "Christian worldview." Saying that we will teach from the perspective of a Christian worldview sounds great. The idea of thinking in terms of a Christian worldview and educating within a Christian worldview framework sounds grandiose and intuitively feels like the right thing to do. Who wouldn't want to teach with the true worldview as your overarching framework? But what does it mean?

As any thoughtful Christian educator knows, be they a teacher, school administrator, professor, parent, or ministry worker, working out what it means in practice is not as easy as it sounds. Indeed, working and thinking in Christian worldview terms sometimes seems unachievable and often frustrating. There are so many articulations of Christian worldview, some of them contradictory or at least at significant variance. Often worldview thinking can feel dogmatic when what you might need in a classroom is freedom to explore ideas. At times, administrators will enforce a particular worldview approach in pedagogy or curriculum, only to leave teachers and professors with no other option than to tick the worldview box in their classrooms and on their plans because implementation is too hard. This is all done with the best of intentions, but can feel empty and unsatisfying for all involved. Worst of all, God and his word can be dishonored by well-meant attempts to work within a Christian worldview approach.

1

Despite these substantial issues that arise when we use the worldview concept, I believe there is a way forward that does not involve scrapping worldview or altering it beyond recognition. There is no silver bullet that will magically resolve the problem. It won't be simple. But it will be worth it. My goal with this book is to provide a way for Christian educators to consider their practices and goals within worldview terms, but without the problems that are often attached to those terms. My goal is to reframe Christian worldview education from a philosophical, theological, and historical standpoint. I want to help educators, ministers of the gospel, pastoral carers, parents, and parachurch workers to rethink Christian worldview and apply it in their vocational settings. What follows is intended to provide a way to think about Christian worldview that really works and that makes sense for Christian education and discipleship in the twenty-first century.

The concept of worldview has a glamorous, checkered, and complex history.[1] In brief, worldview's early exponents included philosophical luminaries such as G. W. F. Hegel (1770–1831) and F. W. J. Schelling (1775–1854). The concept was then taken up by leading Christian thinkers throughout the twentieth century. Worldview language emerged in education settings in the latter part of that century when Christian colleges and Christian schools began to become a major part of the institutional scene. It is now ubiquitous in conservative evangelical and Reformed circles.[2]

---

1. Generally, see David K. Naugle, *Worldview: The History of a Concept* (Downers Grove, IL: IVP Academic, 2002). Also see Simon P. Kennedy, "Christian Worldview and Cosmic War: Contexts and Origins of a Religious Combat Concept," *Church History* 93, no. 1 (2024).

2. A sample: Philip Graham Ryken, *Christian Worldview: A Student's Guide* (Wheaton, IL: Crossway, 2013); Herman Bavinck, *Christian Worldview*, trans. Nathaniel Gray Sutanto, James Eglinton, and Cory C. Brock (Wheaton, IL: Crossway, 2019), hereafter abbreviated as *CW*; David S. Dockery and Trevin Wax, eds., *Christian Worldview Handbook* (Nashville: B&H, 2019); Michael W. Goheen and Craig G. Bartholomew, *Living at the Crossroads: An Introduction to Christian Worldview* (Grand Rapids: Baker Academic, 2008); Albert M. Wolters, *Creation Regained: Biblical Basics for a Reformational Worldview* (Grand Rapids: Eerdmans, 2005); Peter Jones, *The Other Worldview: Exposing Christianity's Greatest Threat* (Bellingham, WA: Kirkdale, 2015); Brian Harris, *The Big Picture: Building Blocks of a Christian World View* (Bletchley: Paternoster, 2015); James W. Sire, *Naming the Elephant: Worldview as a Concept*

Unfortunately, ubiquity does not necessarily equal coherence. The contested nature of the worldview concept points to a weakness in any Christian philosophy of education that relies on this idea. The idea seems intuitively plausible. We all have a view of the world. We all have a framework, or a lens, through which we interpret life. But is this all that a worldview is? And is it enough to simply say that there is a *Christian* worldview and that we should educate from this perspective? I will unpack some of the issues that such a framework can raise for educators and hope that this book provides a way of salvaging the worldview concept.

Let us return to the contested nature of worldview. It is usually healthy for concepts to be contested. However, when concepts are deployed in a normative fashion, as worldview is in Christian education, we ought to be cautious. Normative concepts are powerful, and how they are defined can determine thinking and praxis. In education settings, whether in schools, colleges and universities, or churches, the deployment of normative concepts can wield an influence over who is allowed to teach, who enrolls as a student, what goes into curriculum documents, what content is covered in classes, how the content is presented, and the kinds of authoritative claims that are made in the classroom. The worldview concept underlying these decisions and practices is something of a wax nose, able to be reshaped to suit the whims of the powerful and influential in the institution. Here we have a recipe for worldview tyranny. Even worse, though, is that worldview as it is currently used is an intellectually dubious foundation for education.

(Downers Grove, IL: IVP Academic, 2004); Douglas S. Huffman, ed., *Christian Contours: How a Biblical Worldview Shapes the Mind and Heart* (Grand Rapids: Kregel, 2011); Tawa J. Anderson, W. Michael Clark and David K. Naugle, *An Introduction to Christian Worldview: Pursuing God's Perspective in a Pluralistic World* (Downers Grove, IL: IVP Academic, 2017).

A sample: Summit Ministries, https://www.summit.org; Center for Biblical Worldview, https://www.frc.org/worldview; Worldview Australia, https://www.worldviewaustralia.org; Worldview Academy, https://worldview.org/about; Ezra Institute, https://www.ezrainstitute.ca/about/our-work.

Worldview should be a useful concept for Christian education, but it currently isn't. This is not merely a theological or philosophical problem, off in the realm of the abstract. It has practical implications for educators, church leaders, and administrators. Rethinking worldview should free up teachers to teach their disciplines well, with the ultimate goal being to shape wise and fruitful disciples who are ready to impact God's world. We ought to aim at this, rather than force Christianity and the Bible into every class. Worldview thinking should lead to the Scriptures being treated with dignity in the Christian classroom. Rather than being treated as a proof-text machine, the Bible should be seen as a source of wisdom. Even in education traditions that generally steer clear of this ditch, there are overly simplistic notions of the connection between Christianity and worldview-thinking that frame the task of education. At an institutional level, rethinking worldview should lead to a greater focus on doctrine and catechesis, a prioritizing of great Christian literature, an embracing of rich great books programs, a healthy regard for non-Christian sources and ideas, and an abandonment of bureaucratic markers of "Christianness" like worldview-related learning outcomes.

Naming the Worldview Elephant

Before proceeding with a critique of worldview, we should find out what it is, or at least find out what Christians have said about it. The German jurist Friedrich Julius Stahl defined worldview in such a way as to connect it with philosophy. He wrote in 1846, in a treatise setting forth a Christian philosophy of law, that a worldview is "the apprehension of things in their all-encompassing interconnection according to their highest cause and their final goal."[3] James Orr, a Scottish Presbyterian theologian in the late nineteenth and early twentieth centuries, defined a worldview as "the widest view which the mind can take on things in the effort to grasp them together as

---

3. Friedrich Julius Stahl, *Philosophical Foundations: The Philosophy of Law Volume II*, trans. Ruben Alvarado (Aalten: Wordbridge, 2022), xxi.

a whole from the standpoint of particular philosophy or theology."[4] The Christian worldview was, then, Christianity's "highest point of view, and its view of life connected therewith" brought together in "an ordered whole."[5] Boiled down, Orr held that the Christian worldview is the orderly and rational account of all things from the Christian standpoint, and this is the trajectory that most Christian thinking about worldview has taken.

Several definitions of worldview can also be found in the influential Neo-Calvinist tradition.[6] James Olthuis defines worldview as "a framework or set of fundamental beliefs through which we view the world and our calling and future in it."[7] Albert M. Wolters, in his influential book *Creation Regained*, wrote that a worldview is "the comprehensive framework of one's basic beliefs about things."[8] Both of these definitions focus our attention on the intellectual perspective. Both Olthuis and Wolters think that beliefs have consequences. When worldview is framed in this way, it is readily joined to the practice and philosophy of education. In this understanding of worldview, the intellect informs the rest of life, framing our decisions, actions, relationships, and convictions.[9]

This insight is helpful, to be sure. We are formed and informed by our beliefs, and they set some preconditions for our apprehension of, and interaction with, life. However, as Brad Littlejohn has pointed

---

4. James Orr, *The Christian View of God and the World: As Centring on the Incarnation* (New York: Anson D. F. Randolph, 1893), 3.

5. Orr, *Christian View of God*, 3.

6. Albert Wolters notes the vague definition of worldview offered by Abraham Kuyper and Herman Bavinck: Wolters, "On the Idea of Worldview and Its Relation to Philosophy," in *Stained Glass: Worldviews and Social Science*, ed. Paul A. Marshall, Sander Griffioen, and Richard J. Mouw (Lanham, MD: University Press of America, 1989), 20–21. Wilhelm Dilthey's influence appears to be significant, especially given Bavinck's reliance on him. See, for example, "The Types of World-View and Their Development in Metaphysical Systems," in *Selected Works, Volume VI*, ed. Rudolf A. Makkreel and Frithjof Rodi (Princeton, NJ: Princeton University Press, 2019), 258–62.

7. James H. Olthuis, "On Worldviews," in Marshall, Griffioen, and Mouw, *Stained Glass*, 29.

8. Wolters, *Creation Regained*, 2.

9. See also Simon Smart, "Introduction–Life Visions," in *A Spectator's Guide to Worldviews: Ten Ways of Understanding Life*, ed. Simon Smart (Sydney: Aquila, 2007), 2.

out, we are preconditioned by habits, rituals, and community "much more [than] conceptual systems."[10] A similar critique has been leveled by James K. A. Smith, who has argued that worldview thinking does not provide an adequate account of the way people are formed. According to Smith, worldview thinking fails to account for "the complexity and richness of human persons."[11] In other words, we are not just formed intellectually. The apostle Paul's call to be "transformed by the renewal of your mind" (Rom 12:2) is not a call to have the correct worldview or to properly arrange our intellectual system. Rather, it is a call not to be like those who reject God and debase their minds (Rom 1:28). Instead, we ought to have the mind of Christ, ready to humble ourselves as he did and serve others (Phil 2:5). Humans are creatures with knowledge *and* desires. Nicholas Wolterstorff frames humans as having these two dimensions: "the *assentive* and the *affective*. ... We are deeply attached to some of our beliefs; some of our beliefs are ... formed (in part) by our attachments."[12] In other words, our intellectual beliefs alone do not define us to the extent that these definitions of worldview assume.

Partly in response to these kinds of critiques, some have widened worldview to incorporate the affective aspects of the human person. James Sire has defined a worldview as "a commitment, a fundamental orientation of the heart, that can be expressed as a story or in a set of presuppositions ... about the basic constitution of reality, and that provides the foundation on which we live and move and have our being."[13] Notice his move toward the "orientation of the heart," a welcome one given the inadequacy of intellectualistic approaches. Sire, in another place, states that "a worldview is pretheoretical, below the

---

10. Bradford Littlejohn, *What's Wrong With "Worldview"?* (Moscow, ID: Davenant, 2018), 5.

11. James K. A. Smith, *Desiring the Kingdom: Worship, Worldview, and Cultural Formation,* Cultural Liturgies (Grand Rapids: Baker Academic, 2009), 46.

12. Nicholas Wolterstorff, "On Christian Learning," in Marshall, Griffioen, and Mouw, *Stained Glass,* 67.

13. James W. Sire, *The Universe Next Door: A Basic Worldview Catalogue,* 6th ed. (Downers Grove, IL: IVP Academic, 2020), 6.

conscious mind. ... We think *with* our worldview and *because of* our worldview, not *about* our worldview."[14]

Sire is here acknowledging the entire person in his understanding of worldview, a concession to James K. A. Smith's reorientation of the Christian education project around the insight that we are creatures formed through our loves.[15] Nathaniel Gray Sutanto, Cory Brock, and James Eglinton, drawing on the Dutch theologian Herman Bavinck, also incorporate the heart in their definition of worldview. For them, worldview is "an attempt to unify the self, the head and the heart, on the ground of a primary agreement between religion, science, and philosophy ... [it is] faith seeking understanding."[16] This definition combines the head and the heart, the assentive and the affective.

All of these definitions suffer from a common deficiency: they are vague.[17] How can something so totalistic as a worldview be a mere "attempt" at unifying the different aspects of a person? Surely something more than an attempt is necessary to provide an ontological, spiritual, and epistemological framework by which we interpret all of reality! What about this idea of a "comprehensive framework"? How do we measure how comprehensive it is? If it isn't comprehensive, does it fall short of being a worldview?

Given that it is meant to provide a normative basis for our intellectual, spiritual, and social lives, the worldview concept put forward in these definitions has very little content and almost no philosophical precision. Worldview, it seems, is a conceptual wax nose that can be changed to fit the circumstances and needs of the person wielding it.

This is not the only problem with worldview. As I will explore below, the concept arose in a context very different from our own.

---

14. It is worth considering whether this statement regarding *not* thinking "about our worldview" undermines Sire's entire intellectual project. Sire, *Naming the Elephant*, 143.

15. Smith, *Desiring the Kingdom*; James K. A. Smith, *Imagining the Kingdom: How Worship Works* (Grand Rapids: Baker Academic, 2013); James K. A. Smith, *You Are What You Love: The Spiritual Power of Habit* (Grand Rapids: Brazos, 2016).

16. Nathaniel Gray Sutanto, James P. Eglinton, and Cory Brock, "Editors' Introduction: Herman Bavinck for the Twenty-First Century," in *CW*, 11.

17. Wolterstorff makes this claim in "On Christian Learning," 67.

This means the uses of the worldview concept were originally different from how it ought to be used today when we talk about Christian education. Worldview has been deployed most readily in intellectual combat and apologetics. This is a very different purpose from the one outlined in this book. Rather than build an analytical tool for cultural combat, I will propose a conception of Christian worldview that frames the purpose and practice of Christian education.

The Problem with Christian Worldview

I first noticed a problem with the concept of Christian worldview several years ago when I was researching the political ideas of the Dutch polymath Abraham Kuyper (1837–1920). Kuyper was one of the father figures of the Christian worldview concept, and originally I analyzed his use of worldview in terms of societal structures. According to Kuyper, worldviews were like religious confessions, and they manifested themselves in cultural groupings in society. I was interested in investigating this for its potential as a framework for the governance of religiously diverse societies.[18] However, the more I considered Kuyper's application of his worldview concept to ideas like "Calvinist," "Roman Catholic," and "Liberal," the more I found these worldviews difficult to define and even more difficult to deploy. Kuyper's use of *Weltanschauung* (the German word for worldview) seemed fuzzy at best, and sloppy at worst.

It then dawned on me that worldview language was everywhere in Christian institutions—churches, schools, colleges and universities, and campus ministries—and its typical use here was of the same quality as Kuyper's. Most alarming to me was the realization that I was not exempt from this charge. I used the concept all the time, and I was as fuzzy and sloppy as anyone.

I had no initial need to overcome this difficulty, but the unsatisfactory aspects of the way Christian worldview was articulated became

---

18. Simon P. Kennedy, "Abraham Kuyper: Calvinist Anti-Revolutionary Politician and Political Thinker," *Australian Journal of Politics and History* 61, no. 2 (2015): 169–83; Simon P. Kennedy, "Abraham Kuyper and His Political Thought: Calvinist and Pluralist," *Reformed Theological Review* 72, no. 2 (2013): 73–85.

acute for me when I began teaching in a Christian higher education setting. I found the way that worldview was being deployed in the classroom, the lecture theater, and college marketing materials quite grating. What did we mean by "a Christian worldview perspective" or "teaching from a Christian worldview"? How does having a "Christian worldview" make a difference in learning how to become a good mathematics teacher, historian, or business owner? The setting where it became most frustrating was in the banal world of curriculum documentation. Every course at the college needed to have a learning outcome related to Christian worldview.[19] This raised big questions for me. How do you frame a Christian worldview learning outcome for a course on, for example, ancient Greek and Roman poetry? Or what about a course on the history of World War II? Admittedly, this requirement to have a Christian worldview outcome could be dealt with in a bureaucratic way with little harm done. However, as I was teaching at an institution that prided itself on applying the Christian worldview in every discipline and across every course, the generality and lack of rigor with which the concept was being wielded across the board became a real challenge for me as an educator. I wanted to try and find a way out of, or a way through, the worldview mess. I chose the latter course.

The more I spoke to other people about my concerns, the more I came to believe I was not alone. Christian educators across the primary, secondary, and post-secondary sectors often find the concept difficult. They are invariably passionate about Christian education and often work in Christian institutions. Many of the teachers and professors I encounter at conferences, in professional development sessions, and on university and college campuses are compelled to think of their task in terms of Christian worldview formation and Christian worldview content. And yet they often felt as I did. The idea of a Christian worldview feels intuitively plausible, but when it comes to implementing the idea in the practical context of the classroom or lecture hall, the scope seems extremely limited.

---

19. In Australia, we call "courses" by the name "units." I will use American terminology here.

My own teaching ranges across history, religion, philosophy, and literature, disciplines that offer rich opportunities to bring Christian thinking to bear on many topics. In general, the humanities seem to be a more flexible space for Christian worldview. And yet it remains a challenge, and doubts constantly arise. If you didn't quote the Bible in the class, does it mean you failed to teach from a Christian worldview perspective? Maybe merely having Christian ideas or frameworks should be enough. But how do I know if my ideas are distinctively Christian? How do I know they're not re-engineered liberal secular ideas with a Christian garnish? And what about the possibility of truth being discovered outside the confines of the Christian community? Many cultures with quite varied belief systems have come to scientific, philosophical, and even religious truth without access to a Christian worldview perspective. Presumably, they did so through the use of their God-given reason. This raises the question of what role Christian revelation plays in academic disciplines. Do Christians even have privileged access to intellectual truth? These are the challenges I experienced as an educator, and they seem to resonate with many others across the Christian education sector.

I am not the first person to see problems with the way Christian worldview language is deployed in education. David I. Smith is one scholar who has suggested a different framing for Christian worldview and its relationship to Christian teaching. Smith's solution is to move the conversation away from Christian perspectives on the subject matter and toward the actual practice of teaching. He is most interested in matters related to disposition and environmental factors, like the kinds of sample questions a textbook might contain. Smith draws our attention away from worldview issues in education and toward "the pedagogical process [and] the way the students experience and interpret learning."[20]

James K. A. Smith (who teaches at Calvin University with David I. Smith) has also tried to shift the conversation about Christian

---

20. David I. Smith, *On Christian Teaching: Practicing Faith in the Classroom* (Grand Rapids: Eerdmans, 2018), 3.

education away from the cognitive, rational, and intellectual aspects of Christian worldview by harnessing insights about formation from liturgical theory. For Smith, there is a need to reconsider the goals of Christian education and shift the focus from worldview toward liturgy, by which he means away from the rational and toward the affective. In other words, we should move away from the head and toward the heart when we think about Christian education. "If we," writes Smith, "think about learning in terms of liturgy—pedagogy as liturgy—then ... we need a rearticulation of the end of Christian education."[21]

Both of these contributions have been broadly taken up in Christian education circles in ways that refine the way educators think about integrating Christianity into education. It seems to me that this broad uptake is, in part, a response to the challenges posed by applying worldview thinking in the classroom. Teachers pay lip service to Christian worldview, but it doesn't translate because they feel it doesn't work, and they're looking for other options.

Despite the best efforts of very fine thinkers like David and James Smith, Christian worldview suffers from a lack of real definition. No less a luminary than Nicholas Wolterstorff has brushed aside worldview as a "vague notion."[22] And despite some scholars trying to refine our understanding of worldview and education, the problem that Wolterstorff identified remains. *Contra* a figure like Abraham Kuyper, worldview cannot simply be used to divide up scientific knowledge and different ways of attaining that knowledge.[23] I affirm, with Wolterstorff, that central tenets of a person's beliefs about reality *should not be* arbitrarily abstracted as pillars of their so-called worldview. What does it even mean to do such a thing? No one has yet explained it in a satisfactory way.

---

21. Smith, *Desiring the Kingdom*, 27.

22. Wolterstorff, "On Christian Learning," 67.

23. Abraham Kuyper, *Principles of Sacred Theology*, trans. J. Hendrik de Vries (Grand Rapids: Eerdmans, 1954), 167.

Nevertheless, worldview thinkers often do just this without any justification. All too often, tenets of belief are set apart as crucial to a person's or people's worldview. Some will argue that we can analyze worldviews through answers to set questions. While he doesn't suggest they are sufficient for worldview analysis, N. T. Wright posits the following questions: Who are we? Where are we? What is wrong? and What is the solution? "All cultures," states Wright, "cherish deeprooted beliefs which can in principle be called up to answer these questions."[24] This might be true, so far as it goes. But the obvious problem is which questions to ask. Are these questions, or any other set of questions, the right ones to ask? Why privilege a question about human origins above a question about beauty, for example? Or why privilege epistemology over the question of social justice? And why stop at four questions, or eight? Perhaps there is, in the end, only one question.[25] There is even contention over the *number* of worldview questions people can keep in their heads![26] Not everyone uses this focus on questions to ground their analysis, but the problem is not resolved because the criteria by which someone decides the "ins and outs" of a Christian worldview are still arbitrary and often at odds with the criteria used by other worldview analysts.

The problem is that the concept of worldview is vague. Certain ideas feel important, look neat lined up together, and subsequently get rolled out as if they are definitive for a given person's worldview. It might be argued that if we get these key worldview ideas right, the rest of someone's thinking will sort itself out, and they will start to think in a Christian way. This understanding of worldview, which I will label *deductive*, assumes that starting with the right Christian worldview categories, concepts, and ideas will lead to right thinking and true knowledge. This puts the metaphorical cart before the horse.

---

24. N. T. Wright, *The New Testament and the People of God* (London: SPCK, 1992), 123.

25. See Jones, *The Other Worldview*.

26. C. Fred Smith, *Developing a Biblical Worldview: Seeing Things God's Way* (Nashville: B&H Academic, 2015), 9–10.

Christian worldview thinking is seen as the means, the *way*, that education institutions can offer a Christian education. The most common way this manifests is in the claim to be teaching from a "Christian worldview" perspective, offering correctives to false worldviews. This is a deductive framing of worldview, which starts from high-level first principles, which then (apparently) determine the shape of the rest of someone's view of life. The details of one's life and thinking are then made to fit into the high-level principial worldview markers. But what are these worldview markers (for want of a better term)? It seems that apart from personal intuitions and aesthetic preferences, there is no substantive reason why certain issues or certain questions are central in framing this thing we call a worldview.

These problems with worldview have become more evident in recent years because of our changing cultural context. The original context for the formation and deployment of Christian worldview thinking was quite different from our own. The earliest Christian worldview thinkers of the nineteenth century right down to the apologists and theologians in the late twentieth century all used the concept in contexts where Christianity had cultural currency. The Christian worldview concept was also used in live intellectual combat; it could be used to defend Christian doctrine and fend off hostile attacks from enemies of the faith. At least, that is how its exponents saw it.

Many Christian education institutions emerged in the context of cultural crisis in the 1970s and 1980s, with Christians responding to the sexual revolution and the rising prominence of evolutionary theory with worldview guns blazing. The posture adopted was defensive, and worldview was a defensive weapon. This approach was plausible because Christianity was still a positive cultural force, and bullish worldview-style apologetics could be wielded effectively. But everything has changed. Christianity has moved from being a cultural positive to a cultural negative, and many of these old-style arguments are no longer heard, taken seriously, or comprehended by our pagan culture. We need to respond to this by shifting the way we engage the culture.[27] Just as we need to think differently about worldview, we also need to shift the way we think about education. We cannot simply ward off the evil outside the metaphorical gates, as in the old approach to Christian worldview education. We must also cultivate our own people and disciple our children with a positive vision of Christian worldview. That is what this book puts forward.

The kind of philosophy of worldview education that I outline in this book provides a basis for a proactive Christian approach to education, rather than the defensive one so prevalent from the 1970s onward. I am not saying that we should abandon worldview altogether. Despite the problems with worldview thinking, the solution is not to do away with the concept but to reform it. In reforming worldview, we can also reform our philosophy of Christian education. We are to form our students' worldviews rather than defend prefabricated worldview positions. We are making disciples, not just protecting them. I readily admit that every Christian educator would agree with these statements. Given that that is so, we need to come up with a way of thinking about worldview that fits with this approach, rather than soldiering on with the current method.

The problem that we face as Christian educators and thinkers is that the worldview idea doesn't stand up to philosophical and theological scrutiny if it is framed as a deductive concept. A prominent example of this deductive approach comes from James Sire, in his seminal book *The Universe Next Door*. Sire divides up worldviews according to the answers they give to certain questions: What is prime reality? What is the nature of external reality? What is a human being? What happens when we die? Why is it possible to know anything at all? How do we know what is right and wrong? What is the meaning of human history?[28] Sire then goes on to analyze these worldviews in relation to the Christian worldview. A common way of applying

---

27. Aaron M. Renn, "The Three Worlds of Evangelicalism," *First Things* (February 2022): 1–12.

28. Sire, *Universe Next Door*, 8–9.

this worldview framework would be to take these questions and find out how someone answers them, and then place them in the given worldview box. ("You think there is nothing but physical reality? Materialist it is!")

This kind of worldview analysis has served defensive, combative purposes and has generally faced very little rigorous pushback. The eminent philosopher Raymond Geuss is one exception. Geuss has argued compellingly that worldview talk is evidence of intellectual and cultural weakness. He suggests in an essay on worldview thinking that having a "'total' theory of everything" is "inherently impossible."[29] This critique cuts to the heart of much Christian worldview analysis. For many deductive worldview thinkers, worldview does serve as a total theory of everything. Even worse for many Christian worldview thinkers is his observation that simply turning criticism of worldview-speak around on the critics and saying that they are reasoning from a particular worldview "is so predictable and lame as to be unworthy of consideration."[30] Interestingly, Geuss is not speaking into the Christian conversation about worldview but is rebutting secular accounts of worldview. His is a philosophical critique, not a religious one. However, it is a critique that Christians need to heed.

Is There Hope for Christian Worldview?

I don't want to throw out the concept of Christian worldview altogether. But to make any progress at all, we need a more precise definition of Christian worldview, and I offer this one: a Christian worldview is a true apprehension of reality that is attained through the process of learning about God, the self, and the world. In other words, people have a Christian worldview once they apprehend reality in a way that provides them with holistic insight into right thinking and living. Reality encompasses three elements: God, self, and the rest of creation.

---

29. Raymond Geuss, *Who Needs a World View?* (Cambridge, MA: Harvard University Press, 2020), 33.

30. Geuss, *Who Needs a World View?*, 22. Examples of this type of fallacious argument include Sire, *Naming the Elephant*, 131–32, and Naugle, *Worldview*, 254–55.

The definition affirms the possibility of knowledge of these, and it also affirms the existence and accessibility of reality. Herman Bavinck, in the introduction to his book *Christian Worldview*, puts it like this: "Christianity ... reveals to us a wisdom that reconciles the human being with God and, through this, with itself, with the world and with life."[31]

According to my definition, people have a Christian worldview if they rightly apprehend who God is and who they are, as well as the world around them. Note that I said *a* Christian worldview. I don't believe there is one authoritative Christian worldview. God has an authoritative worldview. But, for reasons I discuss below, I don't believe we have access to this. Therefore, when we talk about a Christian worldview, we are necessarily talking about a subjective worldview. Below, I will show how this subjective view is related to an objective reality. I am not arguing for relativism. As the Dutch missiologist J. H. Bavinck argues, "as soon as God speaks ... the human being gains a firm place to stand."[32] With revelation comes an opportunity for people to connect to objective reality. But I am steering away from any presumption of a monolithic worldview. We all aim at truth, to be sure, and there is one truth. But there are at least as many apprehensions of that truth as there are people, and each of these apprehensions is incomplete and imperfect. We must remain open to the fact that when we are discussing the goals of education, no matter how closely a particular worldview might relate to objective reality, we are talking about a person's worldview rather than the monolithic Christian worldview.

How does this translate in Christian education settings? How does the Christian worldview concept inform Christian philosophies of education? I do not want to use worldview as a way of framing a set of dogmas or determining what subjects ought to be taught and in what fashion. My definition is focused on one thing, and that is

---

31. *CW*, 29.

32. J. H. Bavinck, *Personality and Worldview*, trans. and ed. James Eglinton (Wheaton, IL: Crossway, 2023), 191, hereafter cited as *PW*.

framing the task of Christian education. Until now, Christians have thought about worldview education as the equivalent of working from a finished piece of art, like a mosaic with all of the tiles in place. Or perhaps a better image is that of painting by numbers. The Christian worldview concept seems to provide us with all the "correct answers." All we have to do is get a picture, look at the color guide, and apply the code to the picture. In time, if we follow the instructions carefully, we have a complete and accurate painting. In the same way, with the right "worldview code" our attempts at Christian worldview education are a matter of applying predetermined solutions.

According to this approach, Christian education is carried out deductively, working from higher order principles and overarching ideas down to the metaphorical brass tacks of content in the classroom. Teaching (and learning) in Christian contexts can, as a result, feel like trying to fit information and truth into prefabricated worldview boxes. I want to suggest that worldview education ought to be understood in terms of the construction, or crafting, of a work of art. A Christian worldview is the *aim* of the education process, just as a completed mosaic is the aim of the artistic and construction process that goes into completing a mosaic. Education is akin to the process of crafting a mosaic. It is the process of crafting a worldview.

J. H. Bavinck (1895–1964) provides us with a further illustration of how worldview might work. In his book *Personality and Worldview*, Bavinck argues that worldview is something acquired by a process, a bringing together of the intuitive apprehension of the world (which he calls "worldvision") with a more thought-through, "objective" view of life.[33] Bavinck's translator, James Eglinton, uses a cartographic analogy to help explain this, whereby worldview is a map and we are all mapmakers working out the implications of the Christian faith for our life.[34] J. H. Bavinck's conception of worldview is saddled with some of

---

33. See PW, 34.

34. James Eglinton, "Editor's Introduction," in PW, 11–12. The illustration is also used by Eglinton and his fellow translators in CW, 16–17, 19

the issues outlined above, but this idea that worldview formation constitutes a map-making exercise is useful. Christian education ought to be reimagined as the process of learning truth about God, about ourselves, and God's world. It is like map-making or mosaic-making. If we know God, ourselves, and his world rightly, then we have a Christian worldview. If an education helps people move toward those three things, then you could call this a Christian worldview education. To see this more clearly, I am going to take us back to the fifth century AD.

Of Mosaics and Christian Education

Sometime between AD 430 and 450, the mother of the Roman Emperor Valentinian III built the so-called Mausoleum of Galla Placidia. Located in the ancient town of Ravenna, it may have been a private chapel for the empress, who ruled as regent until AD 437.[35] While it is called a mausoleum, there is not enough evidence to be sure that she built it for her post-death interment. What is certain is that the ceiling of the mausoleum is covered by a stunning set of mosaics. For example, at one end of the chapel there is a lunette depicting two deer drinking from the fountain of life surrounded with intertwined golden acanthus and vines. The vaulted ceiling in front of this lunette is graced by a Chi-Rho symbol encircled by a wreathed crown, itself surrounded by an acanthus and vine pattern. The eye is drawn to the Chi-Rho, the symbol of the triumph of Christ over sin and death, as well as the symbol of Christianity's triumph over the Roman Empire. Galla was probably the patron of the Mausoleum,[36] who provided the financial resources for the mosaic. However, she would have had no practical hand in the work. That would have been left to the artist.

---

35. One scholar has suggested the mausoleum was a burial place for the Gallas' son; see Gillian Mackie, "The Mausoleum of Galla Placidia: A Possible Occupant," *Byzantion* 65, no. 2 (1995): 396–404.

36. The following paragraph relies on Liz James, *Mosaics in the Medieval World: From Late Antiquity to the Fifteenth Century* (Cambridge: Cambridge University Press, 2017), especially chapters 2 and 3. For more on the Mausoleum of Galla Placidia, see 200–202.

The process went something like this. Before any plaster or tiles were applied to the ceiling, there was a great deal of careful planning. The images needed to be mapped out before starting the laying of tiles, possibly by drawing a draft on parchment. A sketch of this would have then been drawn on the masonry, presumably to ensure the proportion of the desired image was appropriate. A further planning step often took place after the application of the initial layers of plaster: underdrawing, or underpainting, which possibly acted as a guide for the artist while also adding depth to the coloring of the image. Underdrawing played an important role in ensuring the artist could work at close range while maintaining the integrity of the image for those viewing it from a distance.

The next step was the laying of *tesserae,* or tiles. Completing a mosaic required the "manual insertion of thousands or millions of small tesserae."[37] The making of these small tiles would have been tedious and extremely time-consuming. Plaster would be applied to

---

37. James, *Mosaics in the Medieval World,* 65.

the area, and the mosaicist would then work steadily away at organizing his tile sets and then placing them. Estimations vary as to how long it took artists to complete the work in question, but some scholars suggest that laying just under one square meter of *tesserae* would take one person roughly a day of work. Others suggest it could have been much slower, which is why it makes sense that mosaicists worked in teams or "workshops." There would likely have been one lead artist overseeing the project, while numerous others worked under his guidance.[38]

The finished product of this process is what we see today on the floor, walls, and ceilings of many ancient and medieval churches, cathedrals, and chapels. The lunette and vault from the Mausoleum of Galla Placidia are just one example of the incredible artistic results of the mosaic artists, who often practiced their craft in the service of Christian patrons like the empress. The images they gifted to the world are often biblical, depicting scenes of creation, redemption, and apocalypse. Often the mosaics of the chapels and churches would climax in an image of Jesus Christ known as the Pantocrator (*pantoktratōr* is a Greek word that can be translated "almighty"). The sacred mosaicist was an artist who created Christian imagery through the complex process of planning and design, preparation, and then craftsmanship.

Mosaic construction provides us with a metaphor for the connection between education and worldview. Think of the mosaic as the worldview and the various mosaicists as those involved in educating others in Christian worldview. This team is creating a beautiful work of art: a Christian worldview. They aren't in charge of the overall picture, and they don't have a clear view of the final design. But they have their instructions and know enough to work on the project.

The mosaic analogy does more than this, though. The artwork we find on the ceiling of the Galla Placidia, and on the many other ancient and medieval churches and chapels scattered across the world, serves

---

38. James, *Mosaics in the Medieval World*, 72–73, 101–5.

a formative purpose for Christian learning and discipleship. These mosaics were not intended to be rational and accurate presentations of the world. They were not presenting a worldview as we might typically think of it. Invariably, the style of art was not precise but was deliberately idealistic, with important themes, symbols, and ideas accentuated for extra impact. The mosaics also had an educative role, not just an aesthetic one. They showed Christians what reality was really about and drew their attention toward the things that mattered most. When people looked up and saw the Pantocrator looming over them, they were being given an image of the cosmos and the cosmic rule of Christ, one that filled their senses, emotions, and imaginations with a sense of the glory and supremacy of their Lord. The point of these images wasn't factual accuracy. The point was that the person saw the cosmos, the heavens and earth, the entirety of reality, in proper perspective.

The project that the builders of the mosaics were working on was essentially the same project as that of Christian worldview education. The aim of both projects is the formation of souls, hearts, and minds by pointing students to Jesus Christ. But notice an important difference, too. Whereas typical worldview education today frames learning and teaching in terms of rational, deductive categories of factual truth or falsity, medieval mosaicists considered their work as concerned not with facts and rational positions but rather with the fundamental orientation of the person toward God. Mosaicists didn't presume to have the final word on how to depict reality or Jesus Christ, nor did they feel the need to have this. They knew they couldn't see everything they needed to see, nor could they see reality clearly. What they could apprehend, the veiled glory of the cosmic Christ, was enough for them to show the world what mattered through their artwork.

The Argument of This Book

This image of the mosaic will serve throughout the rest of the book as a metaphor for Christian education and a Christian worldview. Christian worldview is a constructive project, one that is a partnership between the teacher and student. It aims for a beautiful, finished product with many small pieces making up the whole. Each piece of the mosaic is an aspect of wisdom about God, the student, or his world. And mosaics don't start out as completed works of art. They are pieced together by many people, to the glory of God and his Son.

I noted above that I initially looked for a way out of the problems that worldview presented. However, I realized that worldview language is here to stay, and so is the worldview concept. Therefore, what follows is my attempt to rethink worldview in a way that will serve Christian educators, pastors, and parents.

Chapter 2 offers a historical and cultural analysis of the roots of Christian worldview. The idea emerged in the late nineteenth century through the thought of James Orr and Abraham Kuyper, who were both responding to escalating philosophical, ideological, and religious pluralism. There was a second major emergence of the idea in the 1970s, where the leading thinkers included Francis Schaeffer and Charles Colson. This second emergence is significant in that it set the scene for the contemporary Christian education movement's use of Christian worldview. The chapter will conclude with a diagnostic assessment of the uses of worldview during these periods, noting that worldview emerged as an important idea in the context of cultural and theological crises. I argue that our cultural context is quite different in several important ways, and this signals a need to rethink the use of the worldview concept.

Chapter 3 posits the first part of the solution to the problem set up in chapters 1 and 2. How, then, should we think about Christian worldview? One part of the answer is related to epistemology and theories of learning. Traditional worldview frameworks take a deductive approach to worldview education. That is, Christian educators and institutions think about Christian worldview as a starting point, with first principles and "big-picture" propositional statements shaping the method and content of Christian education. I want to posit an inductive approach to Christian worldview education.

Two figures are worth contrasting at this point as illustrations of the difference between the deductive and inductive approaches. Abraham Kuyper was deductive in his approach to worldview, whereas Herman Bavinck was inductive. Bavinck had an epistemology and understanding of learning that cohered with the inductive worldview concept. James Eglinton puts it nicely in his biography of Bavinck: "Kuyper's vantage point was the big picture. ... He looked down on the world of human beings and their ideas, supremely confident in his own abilities to intervene in and reorder their efforts."[39] Bavinck was a contrasting case, as he "assumed a *starting* rather than a *vantage* point."[40] That starting point would be the place that Bavinck would build from. Bavinck's approach lends itself to seeing education as, recalling the mosaic image, an artistic building project. This chapter provides an alternative model for understanding learning and worldview through the critical realist epistemology of Herman Bavinck. I combine this with aspects of the education theory of Charlotte Mason and propose a theory of learning that is inductive. People learn piece-by-piece and build a body of knowledge, growing up toward big truths about God and the world.

At the core of the Bible's understanding of Christian maturity is wisdom, and I argue that growth in wisdom ought to be a centerpiece of the Christian understanding of education. Chapter 4 posits that Christian formation through growth in wisdom is vital for a robust understanding of worldview. Indeed, the idea of worldview formation ought to be intimately linked to the passing on of wisdom. This chapter proposes a twofold structure to our understanding of wisdom: spiritual and practical. Spiritual wisdom is knowing God and his ways. Practical wisdom is knowing about God's world and one's relation to the things in the world. Both types of wisdom are affirmed by the Bible. They can, and should, be imparted in Christian

---

39. James Eglinton, *Bavinck: A Critical Biography* (Grand Rapids: Baker Academic, 2020), 181.

40. Eglinton, *Bavinck*, 181.

education settings. In sum, this chapter argues that the imparting of practical and spiritual wisdom ought to be at the core of the Christian education project.

The final substantive chapter brings together the theory of learning described in chapter 3 and the centrality of wisdom for Christian education discussed in chapter 4. These two concepts together form a vision of Christian worldview education. Central to this vision is the affirmation of reality. There is an objective, knowable world, made by a loving God who has shown himself to us. Combining Bavinck's understanding of how we learn with the biblical understanding of wisdom shaping what Christians learn (and teach), we arrive at a fresh conception of Christian worldview education. Having a Christian worldview means knowing the truth about reality; it means knowing about God and his world. This is the possession of true wisdom. Therefore, Christian education is the building of a Christian worldview through the imparting of practical and spiritual wisdom.

This book is not meant to be the last word. Like the mosaic, the philosophy of Christian education requires many minds and many hands over many years. To discover where worldview thinking came from and why its current form isn't working anymore, we will now investigate some thinkers on Christian worldview beginning over a century ago.

Chapter 2

How Did We Get Here?
The History of
Christian Worldview

As I mentioned in the previous chapter, the Mausoleum of Galla
Placidia in Ravenna was likely patronized by the empress of
Rome, the mother of Emperor Valentinian III. The images depicted
on the ceiling mosaics range from depictions of Christ as the Good
Shepherd, to figures that appear to be apostles, to the four creatures
of the Apocalypse. The imagery is complex and beautiful. But why
were these particular depictions chosen? What drove the empress or
mosaicists to select this combination of biblical images? We have no
record of the decision-making process for these mosaics. We have
no clear history of why the ceiling of the Mausoleum came to be the
way it is.

The situation is different for the concept of Christian worldview.
We can use the tools of history to ascertain the original aims and
motivations behind the earliest uses of the Christian worldview idea,
and we can observe how the worldview concept has continued to
be deployed. That is the main aim of this chapter. However, this is
not merely an exercise in antiquarianism. The history of Christian
worldview thinking also reveals something important for us today.
The way that worldview thinking has been deployed in the past tells

us something about our fellow Christians from the nineteenth and twentieth centuries that should give us pause: worldview thinking was typically used as a tool of cultural combat rather than as a Christian educational philosophy. The old form of worldview thinking is a square peg in a round hole when applied to Christian education.

Back in 1999, Chuck Colson and Nancy Pearcey wrote about the nature of the putative culture war occurring in America and the West: "The real war is a cosmic struggle between worldviews—between the Christian worldview and the various secular and spiritual worldviews arrayed against it."[1] Here, Colson and Pearcey articulated the potency and importance of the worldview concept within the evangelical Christian ecology. However, few scholars have tackled the history of the concept. One notable exception is David K. Naugle, and another is Molly Worthen.[2] While Naugle's approach is a straightforward conceptual history, unpacking who thought what and when, Worthen's account suggests that the "neo-evangelicals' timely adaption of 'worldview speak' caught on" because of a more general rise of "a presuppositionalist vogue," which can be seen in the emergence of the apologetics of Cornelius Van Til.[3] For Van Til and thinkers who followed him, Christian apologetics should be shaped by the vast differences in presuppositions between Christians and non-believers. Van Til believed there was an underlying battle in apologetic engagement between belief and unbelief, with no possibility of common ground. Worthen places leading worldview thinkers within the context of an increased awareness of the need for evangelical engagement in political and social thought, a need that they understood was based on the differences in presuppositions between believers and unbelievers. I don't think Worthen takes this far enough. Worldview wasn't merely

---

1. Charles Colson and Nancy Pearcey, *How Now Shall We Live?* (Wheaton, IL: Tyndale, 1999), 17.

2. David K. Naugle, *Worldview: The History of a Concept* (Downers Grove, IL: IVP Academic, 2002); Molly Worthen, *Apostles of Reason: The Crisis of Authority in American Evangelicalism* (Oxford: Oxford University Press, 2013).

3. Worthen, *Apostles of Reason*, 260.

a tool of engagement; worldview was a tool of combat. It was (to use intellectual historian Ian Hunter's potent phrase) a "combat concept."[4] To unpack this, and to show how this history should prompt us to carefully consider our own use of the concept, I will first offer an overview of the origins of Christian worldview thinking in the late nineteenth century through the influential writings of James Orr (1844–1913) and Abraham Kuyper (1837–1920). Then, I will deal with the Christian worldview thinking that emerged in the 1960s and 1970s, led by Francis Schaeffer (1912–1984) and carried on by others like Pearcey and Colson. Both took place in the context of escalating cultural and religious pluralism, in which conservative Christians displayed a heightened sense of ideological conflict. In this environment, worldview thinking became a tool for differentiation from, and contention with, the "other." In short, the concept of Christian worldview emerged as a combat concept in contexts of perceived cultural crisis.

From German Idealism to James Orr

The concept of "worldview," "world-and-life-view," or *Weltanschauung* has a history that stretches back to the German idealists.[5] Immanuel Kant (1724–1804) deployed the term *Weltanschauung* in his *Critique of Judgment* (1790), when he said that the presence of a "supersensible" faculty of the human mind is complemented by an appropriation and explanation of the world based on the individual's experience and consciousness. Kant called this "the intuition of the world (*weltanschauung*)."[6] In Martin Heidegger's words, Kant is referring to "world-intuition in the sense of contemplation of the world given to the senses ... a beholding of the world as simple apprehension of nature."[7]

---

4. Ian Hunter, "Secularization: The Birth of a Modern Combat Concept," *Modern Intellectual History* 12, no. 1 (2015): 3–4.

5. For a summary of the early history of the worldview idea, see Naugle, *Worldview*, 68–107.

6. Immanuel Kant, *Critique of Judgement*, ed. Nicholas Walker (Oxford: Oxford University Press, 2007).

7. Martin Heidegger, *The Basic Problems of Phenomenology*, trans. Albert Hofstader (Indiana University Press, 1988), 4.

F. W. J. Schelling (1775–1854) reiterated Kant's idea in his *System of Transcendental Idealism* (1800), when he attempted to explain how people can see the same world from different perspectives. "I draw the concept of intelligence," writes Schelling, "solely from myself, an intelligence that I am to recognize as such must stand under the same conditions in intuiting the world (*Weltanschauung*) as I do myself."[8]

G. W. F. Hegel (1770–1831) would later move the idea of worldview a step toward what was eventually articulated by the early Christian worldview advocates. In his *Lectures on the Philosophy of History* (delivered between 1822 and 1830), Hegel described, for example, the South Asian way of understanding the cosmos, humanity and human nature, and the divine as "a general idea of the Indian world-view (*Weltanschauung*)."[9] Further, in his description of the North American framework of religious pluralism and sectarianism, Hegel describes those advocating for religious freedom and plurality as "maintaining that everyone may have his own world view, and thus his own religion as well."[10]

This German idealist background is significant for how the worldview concept was framed in conservative Christian circles in the late nineteenth century, especially by the Scottish theologian James Orr. Orr's spiritual formation was evangelical, and he was involved in the United Presbyterian Church from his youth. His studies at the University of Glasgow focused on "mental philosophy." Orr's theology moved in a liberalizing direction (relative to his conservative denomination) through the 1880s, although in the end Orr sided with conservative Reformed and fundamentalist thinkers, as evidenced by him being a key contributor to *The Fundamentals* series in the early

---

8. F. J. W. Schelling, *System of Transcendental Idealism (1800)*, trans. Peter Heath (University Press of Virginia, 1978), 164.

9. G. W. F. Hegel, *Lectures on the Philosophy of History*, trans. Ruben Alvarado (Aalten, the Netherlands: Wordbridge, 2011), 128.

10. Hegel, *Lectures on the Philosophy of History*, 78.

twentieth century.[11] His engagement with questions relating to the connections between Christianity, modernism, and culture was at the core of his work as a theologian.[12] Michelle Sanchez shows that Orr was "in many ways a Kant aficionado" who "altered the [worldview] concept to fit his particular apologetic aims."[13] Further, he was, to use Geoffrey Treloar's phrase, "probably the most extensively published evangelical writer of the era."[14]

When Orr published *The Christian View of God and the World* in 1893, he mentioned the worldview concept in the second paragraph. Orr wrote that when he used the phrase "Christian view of the world," he was using an idea found commonly in German idealism: "It is the word 'Weltanschauung.' "[15] This word, according to Orr, denotes "the widest view which the mind can take of things and the effort to grasp them together as a whole" from a particular philosophical or theological viewpoint.[16] Speaking, therefore, of a "Christian view of the world" implies that Christianity has a viewpoint that, "when developed, constitutes an ordered whole."[17] There was no question in Orr's mind that Christianity has within itself a "view of things, which has a character, coherence, and unity of its own."[18]

---

11. On *The Fundamentals*, see George M. Marsden, *Fundamentalism and American Culture* (New York: Oxford University Press, 2006), 118–23. Orr's contributions were "The Virgin Birth of Christ," in *The Fundamentals*, vol. 1 (Chicago: Testimony, 1910), 7–20; "Science and the Christian Faith," in *The Fundamentals*, vol. 4 (Chicago: Testimony, 1910), 91–104; "The Early Narratives of Genesis," in *The Fundamentals*, vol. 6 (Chicago: Testimony, 1911), 85–97; "Holy Scripture and Modern Negations," in *The Fundamentals*, vol. 9 (Chicago: Testimony, 1912), 31–47.

12. Glen G. Scorgie, *A Call for Continuity: The Theological Contribution of James Orr* (repr., Vancouver, BC: Regent College, 2004), 20–46.

13. Michelle C. Sanchez, "Orr and Kant: An Analysis of the Intellectual Encounter Behind 'The Christian Worldview,' " *Scottish Journal of Theology* 74, no. 2 (2021): 105.

14. Geoffrey R. Treloar, *The Disruption of Evangelicalism: The Age of Torrey, Mott, McPherson, and Hammond* (Downers Grove, IL: IVP Academic, 2017), 77.

15. James Orr, *The Christian View of God and the World: As Centring on the Incarnation* (New York: Anson D. F. Randolph, 1893), 3.

16. Orr, *Christian View of God*, 3.

17. Orr, *Christian View of God*, 3.

18. Orr, *Christian View of God*, 17–18.

This allowed Orr to do three things. First, Orr believed he could systematize Christianity by thinking it through as a *Weltanschauung*: "It enables me to deal with Christianity in its entirety or as a system."[19] Second, Orr believed that addressing the Christian faith as a worldview allowed him to give reasonable theoretical justifications for the claims of Christianity, both those that are specific and those that are more systematic.[20] Finally, and most crucially for our purposes, Orr believed he could more readily contrast the Christian worldview with "counter-theories and speculations." Here, Orr turned the Christian worldview into a combat concept.[21]

Orr saw Christianity as vulnerable to attack from alien forces, and we will see below that Kuyper shared this sentiment. In a remarkable passage, Orr says, "No one ... whose eyes are open to the signs of the times, can fail to perceive that if Christianity is to be effectually defended from the attacks made upon it, it is the comprehensive method which is rapidly becoming the more urgent."[22] Theological liberalism, the moral aestheticism of the Romantics, and Darwinism would appear to be prime opponents for Orr.[23] However, he asserted that the kinds of opposition that Christianity faced were no longer merely doctrinal or focused on the natural sciences. Rather, the conflict "extends to the whole manner of conceiving of the world, and of man's place in it, the manner of conceiving of the entire system of things, natural and moral, of which we form a part. It is no longer an opposition of detail, but of principle."[24] Orr clearly saw his groundbreaking use of worldview as a tool of apologetics, of defense and debate, and as the method by which "the attack [on Christianity] can

19. Orr, *Christian View of God*, 4.

20. Orr, *Christian View of God*, 18.

21. Scorgie, *Call for Continuity*, 53.

22. Orr, *Christian View of God*, 4.

23. Charles Taylor, *A Secular Age* (Cambridge, MA: Belknap Press, 2007), 352–98; Owen Chadwick, *The Secularization of the European Mind* (Cambridge: Cambridge University Press, 1975), 229–49.

24. Orr, *Christian View of God*, 4.

most successfully be met."[25] This early understanding of Christian worldview set up the apologetic use of *Weltanschauung* as combative from the very beginning. Orr wielded worldview as a weapon in "the battle between faith and unbelief."[26] This combative method was carried on by Abraham Kuyper.

Kuyper and the Neo-Calvinists

Kuyper rode a wave that started with the constitutional revolutions of the mid-nineteenth century, a ride that continued until he became the prime minister of Holland. Born in 1838, Kuyper worked his way toward a pastorate in the national Reformed Church, gaining his doctorate along the way. He started his pastoral life as a theological liberal before having something of a conversion experience upon seeing the authentic and simple Reformed Christianity of the faithful in his backwater parish. It was these lower-class Calvinists, the "little people," as Kuyper called them, that formed the backbone of a burgeoning political movement in Holland.

Disenchantment with the aftermath of the French Revolution and the overturning of the *ancien régime* on the part of these conservative Calvinists, a sentiment powerfully articulated by Guillaume Groen van Prinsterer (1801–1876) in the mid-nineteenth century, led to the organization of the first mass party in Holland.[27] Groen was something of an ideological grandfather to Kuyper and the Anti-Revolutionary Party (ARP), which was formalized in 1879. The ARP formed its first coalition government in 1888, and again in 1901, with Kuyper being the prime minister in the latter government.[28] Kuyper

---

25. Orr, *Christian View of God*, 4.

26. Orr, *Christian View of God*, 398.

27. Guillaume Groen van Prinsterer, *Unbelief and Revolution*, trans. Harry Van Dyke (Bellingham, WA: Lexham, 2018). On Groen, see Harry Van Dyke, *Challenging the Spirit of Modernity: A Study of Groen van Prinsterer's* Unbelief & Revolution (Bellingham, WA: Lexham, 2019); Gerrit J. Schutte, *Groen van Prinsterer: His Life and Work*, trans. Harry Van Dyke (Neerlandia, AB: Inheritance, 2016).

28. Kuyper's articulation of the party's platform is found in Abraham Kuyper, *Our Program: A Christian Political Manifesto* (Bellingham, WA: Lexham, 2015).

also achieved remarkable things in journalism and education, particularly in his founding of, and professorship at, the Free University of Amsterdam.[29]

Kuyper was the very embodiment of Aristotle's active life, and yet he is best known for his ideas. He delivered the 1898 Stone Lectures at Princeton Theological Seminary, where he articulated a case for Calvinist Christianity as a worldview. In the lectures, Kuyper argued that Calvinism represented a comprehensive system of belief about all aspects of life, from theology proper to art, to politics, and to history.[30]

Kuyper's explicit project in his *Lectures* is to provide a framework for the "consistent defense for Protestant nations against encroaching and overwhelming Modernism."[31] What is this behemoth of modernism? Kuyper describes it as an "all-embracing life system" that is "wrestling with" Christianity and that originated with the French Revolution.[32] The "life-system" of Modernism is "bound to build a world of its own," in contrast with those who are "bent on saving the 'Christian heritage.' "[33]

Two things are notable here. The first is that Kuyper is using the phrase "life-system" rather than "worldview" or "life- and worldview" advisedly, as he notes in a footnote that "my American friends ... told me that the shorter phrase *life system* ... is often used in the same sense" in North America.[34] "Life-system" and "worldview" are used

---

29. The best biography is James D. Bratt, *Abraham Kuyper: Modern Calvinist, Christian Democrat* (Grand Rapids: Eerdmans, 2013). See also Richard J. Mouw, *Abraham Kuyper: A Short and Personal Introduction* (Grand Rapids: Eerdmans, 2011); Jan de Bruijn, *Abraham Kuyper: A Pictorial Biography*, trans. Dagmare Houniet (Grand Rapids: Eerdmans, 2014).

30. See, generally, Peter S. Heslam, *Creating a Christian Worldview: Abraham Kuyper's Lectures on Calvinism* (Grand Rapids: Eerdmans, 1998).

31. Abraham Kuyper, *Calvinism: Six Lectures Delivered in the Theological Seminary at Princeton* (New York: Fleming H. Revell, 1899). The version cited here will be Abraham Kuyper, *Lectures on Calvinism* (Peabody, MA: Hendrickson, 2008). Quotation is from page 4.

32. Kuyper, *Lectures*, 3–4; George Harinck, "Herman Bavinck and the Neo-Calvinist Concept of the French Revolution," in *Neo-Calvinism and the French Revolution*, ed. James Eglinton and George Harinck (London: T&T Clark, 2014), 13–30.

33. Kuyper, *Lectures*, 3.

34. Kuyper, *Lectures*, 3.

interchangeably throughout his *Lectures*.[35] Second, and perhaps most significant, is the setting up of a "wrestle," of two systems in "mortal combat," of "a struggle for principles."[36] Here we can see a further example of Christian worldview as a combat concept, as Kuyper put forth Calvinism as the life system equipped to spar with insidious modernism.[37]

Also, as he states in his first lecture, Kuyper is not simply talking about Calvinism in a sectarian or confessional sense.[38] He understands Calvinism to be a comprehensive "form for human life, to furnish human society with a different method of existence, and to populate the world of the human heart with different ideals and conceptions."[39] It is "the creator of a world of human life entirely of its own."[40] In other words, Calvinism is a *Weltanschauung* that is capable of bolstering the "vague conception of Protestantism" with a "unity of starting point and life system."[41] This kind of life-system, or worldview, is necessary, suggests Kuyper, because without it Protestants "must lose the power to maintain our independent position, and our strength for resistance must ebb away" in face of the challenges of modernism.[42] Christians will not be able to successfully defend their position except "by placing, in opposition to all of this, *a life and worldview of your own, founded as firmly on the base of your own principle.*"[43] His central claim is, then, that the "Calvinistic principle" provides the grounds for "the defence of Christianity, principle over against principle, and world-view over against world-view."[44]

---

35. Something he notes in the footnote in Kuyper, *Lectures*, 3.

36. Kuyper, *Lectures*, 3.

37. Kuyper, *Lectures*, 4.

38. Kuyper, *Lectures*, 5.

39. Kuyper, *Lectures*, 9.

40. Kuyper, *Lectures*, 14.

41. Kuyper, *Lectures*, 10.

42. Kuyper, *Lectures*, 10.

43. Kuyper, *Lectures*, 173. Emphasis is original.

44. Kuyper, *Lectures*, 174. Cf. Kuyper, *Lectures*, 117, for his introduction of the idea of the antithesis between belief and unbelief.

Kuyper is here clearly articulating a theory of Christian world-view as a combat concept. There is, according to Kuyper, an opposition that needs to be reckoned with and a darkening world that Christians are speaking into. For Kuyper, the Christian worldview is the solution.[45] Kuyper's politics and his worldview philosophy are set against the backdrop of cultural change in the late nineteenth and early twentieth centuries. His political and ecclesial activities, along with his writings, are interventions in a context where conservative, traditional Reformed Christianity was becoming marginalized. The context for Kuyper's assertions about the distinctiveness of the Calvinist confession and worldview is one of increasing ideological and religious pluralism, which came as something of a crisis for traditional, Reformed Christians in Holland.[46]

After Kuyper, the Neo-Calvinist branch of worldview thinking continued in Holland and North America. Dutch thinkers such as Herman Dooyeweerd (1894–1977) and D. H. Vollenhoven (1892–1978), both professors at the Free University of Amsterdam, applied Kuyper's worldview ideas across philosophy and law in the early and mid-twentieth century, although in a more heuristic and less combative manner.[47] This Neo-Calvinist influence was carried to North America and embedded at Calvin College in Grand Rapids. Leading Kuyperian faculty at Calvin included William Harry Jellema (1893–1982) and H. Evan Runner (1916–2002), both of whom were professors of philosophy.

The Dutch Reformed influence on evangelical and Reformed worldview thinking eventually bore substantial fruit in the 1970s,

---

45. Cf. Harinck, "Herman Bavinck and the Neo-Calvinist Concept," 19–20.

46. On Kuyper's role, see Bratt, Abraham Kuyper, 149–72; more generally, see John Halsey Wood, Going Dutch in the Modern Age: Abraham Kuyper's Struggle for a Free Church in the Netherlands (Oxford: Oxford University Press, 2013); Kennedy, "Abraham Kuyper: Calvinist Anti-Revolutionary Politician"; Bratt, Abraham Kuyper, 68–70.

47. D. H. Vollenhoven, Het Calvinime en de Reformatie van de Wijsbegeerte (Amsterdam: H. J. Paris, 1933); Herman Dooyeweerd, New Critique of Theoretical Thought, 4 vols. (Jordan Station, ON: Paideia, 1984); Herman Dooyeweerd, Vernieuwing en bezinning. Om het reformatorisch grondmotief (Zutphen: J. B. van den Brink, 1963).

partly through the influence of Cornelius Van Til (1895–1987). Van Til moved from Holland to the United States as a child and attended Calvin before going to Princeton for graduate studies. The influence of Kuyper on Van Til is explicit at key points, and he worked out the implications of Kuyper's stark division of worldviews in his method of presuppositional apologetics.[48] Van Til took Kuyper's assertion that there are two kinds of science, one Christian and one not, and applied it to theological epistemology.[49] "In the last analysis," asserts Van Til in his influential work *The Defense of the Faith*, "we shall have to choose between two theories of knowledge."[50]

Van Til played an important role in Francis Schaeffer's formation. Schaeffer initially studied at Westminster Theological Seminary in Philadelphia. Westminster was founded as a break-away from Princeton Theological Seminary, defining itself as a conservative, "confessional" institution over-against the "modernism" of Princeton. It was formed under the leadership of J. Gresham Machen (1881–1937), who played a leading role in the "fundamentalist-modernist controversy."[51] It was in this same context of controversy that Van Til joined Machen as part of the burgeoning faculty of Westminster and would go on to wield a substantial influence over Schaeffer. Schaeffer was formed by this cultural and religious background of crisis, controversy, and combat for the truth in the public square.

Francis Schaeffer and the Schaefferians

The 1960s and 1970s, when Schaeffer was developing his public ministry, was ripe for worldview combat. Christians were confronted with the Sexual Revolution, the civil rights movement, the Vietnam War,

---

48. Cornelius Van Til, *The Defense of the Faith*, 3rd ed. (Phillipsburg, NJ: P&R, 1967), 260–66.

49. Abraham Kuyper, *Principles of Sacred Theology*, trans. J. Hendrik de Vries (Grand Rapids: Eerdmans, 1954), 167.

50. Van Til, *Defense of the Faith*, 34.

51. On Machen more generally, see D. G. Hart, *Defending the Faith: J. Gresham Machen and the Crisis of Conservative Protestantism in Modern America* (Baltimore: Johns Hopkins University Press, 1994).

and the general shift away from traditional cultural norms through popular and hippie culture.[52] Schaeffer's use of worldview as a combat concept was honed in this context. He founded L'Abri (French for "the shelter") with his wife Edith in Switzerland in 1955 as a study center for those seeking and exploring faith and meaning in the postmodern West. It was through this ministry to seekers and doubters that his profile as a public intellectual grew. Schaeffer returned temporarily to the United States in the late 1960s to publish his books and speak to packed-out audiences at colleges, universities, and churches, and went on to make documentaries and influence thousands of Christians with his critiques of Western culture.[53]

Schaeffer's influences included Kuyper and the presuppositional apologetics of Van Til, who was particularly apposite to his purposes, with his stark division between Christian belief and unbelief and his view of the impact of the fall on the intellect.[54] For Schaeffer, this division formed the basis of the worldview combat concept (even if he disagreed with Van Til over the status of the non-believer's knowledge about the world and God).[55] The idea of different worldviews is found throughout Schaeffer's writings and especially provides a framework for his cultural and political analysis, which pits the Christian worldview against all others.[56]

---

52. Mark A. Noll, *A History of Christianity in the United States and Canada*, 2nd ed. (Grand Rapids: Eerdmans, 2019), 414–31; Brian Stanley, *Christianity in the Twentieth Century: A World History* (Princeton, NJ: Princeton University Press, 2018), 118–24; Darren Dochuk, *From Bible Belt to Sunbelt: Plain-folk Religion, Grassroots Politics, and the Rise of Evangelical Conservatism* (New York: W. W. Norton, 2012).

53. Edith Schaeffer, *L'Abri* (Wheaton, IL: Tyndale House, 1969), 106–7; Barry Hankins, *Francis Schaeffer and the Shaping of Evangelical America* (Grand Rapids: Eerdmans, 2008), 74–79.

54. Van Til, *Defense of the Faith*, 43–44. Cf. Kuyper's distinction between believing and unbelieving science in Kuyper, *Lectures*, 125–26; Abraham Kuyper, *Principles of Sacred Theology*, 167.

55. Cornelius Van Til, "A Letter from Cornelius Van Til to Francis Schaeffer," March 11, 1969, https://opc.org/OS/html/V6/4d.html. Cf. Francis Schaeffer, *The Complete Works of Francis Schaeffer*, 5 vols. (Wheaton, IL: Crossway, 1982), 1:7–9.

56. For a sample of his uses of worldview, see Schaeffer, *Complete Works*, 1:24, 46; 4:105.

"People function," according to Schaeffer, "on the basis of their world-view more consistently than even they themselves may realize."[57] According to Schaeffer, ideas drive action and the course of history. Therefore, divisions between worldviews are founded upon thought. In the opening of his documentary film *How Should We Then Live?* (1976), he says, "There is a flow to history and culture ... rooted in what people think, and what they think will determine how they act."[58] Ideas drive ethics, and ethics drive culture.[59] Schaeffer constructs this framework for understanding the flow of culture by presenting different ways or systems of thought as worldviews. These worldviews are in tension with one another, and Schaeffer paints them as vying for dominance across history. One example of this is Schaeffer's juxtaposition of the ancient Roman worldview, which the apostle Paul spoke into with the Christian worldview.[60] This juxtaposition is another example of using worldview as a combat concept. In the final words of *How Should We Then Live?*, Schaeffer says that "the problem is not outward things," by which he means that it is not the material that matters. Rather, it is ideas: "The problem is having the right worldview, and acting upon it; the worldview that gives men and women the truth of what is."[61]

In his *A Christian Manifesto* (1981), Schaeffer carries on his analysis from *How Shall We Then Live?* He frames the problem of modern America in terms of a move away from a Christian worldview toward a non-Christian one.[62] The setting for the *Manifesto* is the rise of the Moral Majority, the emergence of a "Religious Right" in American politics, and a growing sense among traditional Christians of a

---

57. Schaeffer, *Complete Works*, 5:252.

58. Francis Schaeffer, "01 - The Roman Age," https://www.youtube.com/watch?v=Np-PMMb50QcE, at 1:07.

59. Francis Schaeffer, *Complete Works*, 5:209.

60. Francis Schaeffer, "10 - Final Choices," https://www.youtube.com/watch?v=jJ4sD-k4LkAM, at 21:55.

61. Schaeffer, "10 - Final Choices," https://www.youtube.com/watch?v=jJ4sDk4LkAM, at 25:26; see also Schaeffer, *Complete Works*, 5:252.

62. Schaeffer, *Complete Works*, 5:423.

liberalization of society. Mark Noll sensibly puts the turning point of this shift in consciousness at *Roe v. Wade*, the Supreme Court decision that legalized abortion nationwide in 1973, and Schaeffer is in many ways a leading figure in the evangelical and conservative Christian reaction to *Roe*, pushing back against a pervasive "secular humanism."[63] According to Schaeffer, these "world views stand in total and complete antithesis to each other in content but also in their natural results" in society and government.[64] They are in combat, and society is being dragged away, says Schaeffer, by the pagan, materialist worldview: "What we must understand is that the two world views really do bring forth with inevitable certainty ... total differences in regard to society, government, and law. There is no way to mix these two total world views. They are separate entities that cannot be synthesized."[65]

This language helped mobilize the conservative evangelical constituency, who looked to Schaeffer as a cultural commentary guru.[66] His analysis suggested that the "loss of the Christian consensus" had given way to dominance by a pagan, humanist elite.[67]

Elsewhere, in *Whatever Happened to the Human Race?* (1983, coauthored with C. Everett Koop), Schaeffer asserts that "humanism has replaced Christianity," resulting in a "change [to] people's view of themselves and their attitudes towards other human beings."[68] This shift in consensus, in dominant worldviews, resulted in an increase in "personal cruelty" along the lines of immoral genetic research, child abuse, euthanasia, and abortion.[69] All of this is a sign that

---

63. Mark A. Noll, *The Scandal of the Evangelical Mind* (Grand Rapids: Eerdmans, 1994), 170. Cf. Schaeffer, *Complete Works*, 5:220. On the rise in "family values" politics at this time, see Seth Dowland, *Family Values and the Rise of the Christian Right* (Philadelphia: University of Pennsylvania Press, 2015); Daniel Williams, *God's Own Party: The Making of the Christian Right* (Oxford: Oxford University Press, 2010), 139.

64. Schaeffer, *Complete Works*, 5:424.

65. Schaeffer, *Complete Works*, 5:425.

66. Williams, *God's Own Party*, 140–42.

67. Schaeffer, *Complete Works*, 5:224; cf. 5:284.

68. Schaeffer, *Complete Works*, 5:284.

69. Schaeffer, *Complete Works*, 5:286–308.

the Christian worldview has been abandoned and replaced with a worldview that rejects the tenets of the sanctity of human life and the political freedoms that the Christian culture developed.[70] In the final analysis, argued Schaeffer, "there are only two alternatives ... first, imposed order [by humanist elites] or, second, our society once again affirming ... God's revelation in the Bible and His revelation through Christ."[71] To return to "God's revelation" would be nothing other than having "the right world view," a return that would result in a rejection of the imposed pagan order.[72] Schaeffer unquestionably deployed worldview, and the idea of a Christian worldview over against other worldviews, as a combat concept in a heightened atmosphere of culture war.

The legacy of Schaeffer's use of worldview as a combat concept is significant, and one need only look at two prominent evangelical writers to see the way this has played out. James Sire (1933–2018), at the time an editor at InterVarsity Press, was present at Schaeffer's 1968 lectures at Wheaton College. Sire convinced Schaeffer to allow him to transcribe the recorded lectures into a book.[73] He had facilitated the publication of some of Schaeffer's previous work, but this began a close working relationship where Sire had input into the prose and shape of Schaeffer's work.[74] Only eight years later, Sire himself penned one of the most widely read books on Christian worldview, *The Universe Next Door* (1976). The book is now into a sixth edition. In his preface to the fifth edition, Sire explained that the original audience of the book was "Christians in the mid-1970s," and the book was "designed to help them identify why they felt so 'out of it'" in the college and university context when "their professors

70. Schaeffer, *Complete Works*, 5:245–50.
71. Schaeffer, *Complete Works*, 5:250.
72. Schaeffer, *Complete Works*, 5:252.
73. Hankins, *Francis Schaeffer*, 109.
74. Hankins, *Francis Schaeffer*, 80–81.

assumed the truth of ideas they deemed odd or even false."[75] The study was designed to help people see and understand "the differences between the Christian worldview and the various worldviews that either stemmed from Christianity ... or countered Christianity at its very intellectual roots."[76] Here we see an undoubtedly Schaefferian focus on ideas being foundational for the analysis of difference, but also the assumption that worldviews can be essentially explained by examining answers to intellectual questions.[77]

A similar approach, though one more in tune with Schaeffer's cultural and political use of worldview as a combat concept, is that of Nancy Pearcey (1952–), mentioned at the start of this chapter in connection with her work alongside Charles Colson (1931–2012). Pearcey studied under Schaeffer at L'Abri, studied at the Kuyper-influenced Institute for Christian Studies in Canada, and held a chair in Schaeffer's name at the World Journalism Institute.[78] Together with Colson, Pearcey penned the words, "The world is divided not so much by geographic boundaries as ... by worldviews."[79] This is found in a book whose title obviously harkens back to Schaeffer, *How Now Shall We Live?*, and features him in the dedication. "The culture war" is not, according to Colson and Pearcey, just about babies, sex, and drugs. Rather, the "real war is a cosmic struggle between worldviews—between the Christian worldview and the various secular and spiritual worldviews arrayed against it."[80] Like Schaeffer, Colson and Pearcey argue that ideas drive action and that adopting "a false worldview" has catastrophic results for individuals.[81] However, the combat at a societal and cultural level is their main interest. This combat is not

---

75. James W. Sire, *The Universe Next Door: A Basic Worldview Catalogue*, 6th ed. (Downers Grove, IL: IVP Academic, 2020), 11.

76. Sire, *Universe Next Door*, 11.

77. An approach he nuanced in James W. Sire, *Naming the Elephant: Worldview as a Concept* (Downers Grove, IL: IVP Academic, 2004).

78. http://www.pearceyreport.com/about.php.

79. Colson and Pearcey, *How Now Shall We Live?*, 19.

80. Colson and Pearcey, *How Now Shall We Live?*, 17.

81. Colson and Pearcey, *How Now Shall We Live?*, 477.

merely based on a misunderstanding, but is a "clash of worldviews that is changing the face of American society."[82] Pearcey deepens this conception of worldview as a combat concept in her later work, stating that "the purpose of worldview studies is nothing less than to liberate Christianity from its cultural captivity, unleashing its power to transform the world."[83] To do this, states Pearcey, "we need to become utterly convinced that, as Francis Schaeffer said, Christianity is not merely religious truth, it is total truth."[84] Pearcey not only quotes Schaeffer here but is employing worldview as a combat concept as her mentor and hero once did.

This approach to cultural critique and worldview thinking has continued to find its way into numerous influential books and teaching series. A prominent example of the latter is Focus on the Family's *The Truth Project* (2008), which purports to offer worldview-related insights that will transform how people think and then live. The solution to living in a hostile world is a repaired worldview, a Christian worldview. At times, it seems like the Christian worldview might be replacing the gospel itself! Even though this isn't ultimately the goal of *The Truth Project*, it can seem as though intellectual assent to the correct worldview is the aim.[85] In the series, the Christian worldview combats the wrong view of biology, the wrong view of epistemology, the wrong view of the American founding; and it "transforms people." The influence of Schaeffer's combat concept is evident.

A Cautionary Tale

Now that we have seen *how* it emerged, it remains to try and explain *why* this worldview combat concept emerged. I have suggested that the context was cultural conflict and perceived crisis. But what was the motivation for using worldview in particular? I propose that

---

82. Colson and Pearcey, *How Now Shall We Live?*, 26.

83. Nancy R. Pearcey, *Total Truth: Liberating Christianity from Its Cultural Captivity* (Wheaton, IL: Crossway, 2005), 17.

84. Pearcey, *Total Truth*, 18.

85. An error astutely critiqued by J. H. Bavinck; see *PW*, 170.

Christians who first used the worldview concept in the nineteenth century, as well as those who did again in the 1970s and on into today, did so to fill a vacuum left by the de-Christianization of Western society. Up until the nineteenth century, Christianity surrounded every aspect of life, such that even the most undevout were still embraced by a lived experience where Christianity required no justification. When the de-Christianization of society began to affect the church more directly through the emerging theological liberalism, worldview thinking was part of the response.

In his 1939 lectures that became *The Idea of a Christian Society*, T. S. Eliot posited some points that help explain the kind of shift in conditions that evangelicals and other Christians might have been responding to during the periods under scrutiny here. Eliot said that a society ceased to be Christian when Christian "religious practices have been abandoned, when behavior ceases to be regulated by reference to Christian principle, and when in effect prosperity in this world for the individual or for the group has become the sole conscious aim."[86] Eliot also described the tensions of "leading a Christian life in a non-Christian society."[87] Christians in the early twentieth century were, according to Eliot, implicated "in a network of institutions from which we cannot dissociate ourselves ... the operation of which appears no longer neutral, but non-Christian."[88] This results in a pressure to become "more and more de-Christianized by all sorts of unconscious pressure" because "paganism holds all the most valuable advertising space."[89] Not only that, but in a liberal society, Eliot suggests, Christians are more vulnerable to these cross-pressures due to being a tolerated minority.

I am not suggesting that Eliot's diagnosis is correct. Rather, I wonder whether he is describing something like the experience of

---

86. T. S. Eliot, *Christianity and Culture* (repr., New York: Harcourt, Brace, 1960), 9–10.
87. Eliot, *Christianity and Culture*, 17.
88. Eliot, *Christianity and Culture*, 17.
89. Eliot, *Christianity and Culture*, 18.

Kuyper and Orr, and then their latter-day American followers. It is the experience of a cultural shift, where all of the ground seems to have moved from under one's feet and the sudden need arises to explain and justify yourself not only to others, but also to yourself. The Christian cultural milieu changed, such that Christians needed to provide what they thought was a systematic explanation of their own understanding of life and meaning.

This possibility is developed by the philosopher Raymond Geuss. In his book *Who Needs a World View?*, Geuss describes a worldview, but not as a grand scientific and systematic theory of reality, which is often how Christians and others imagine it. Rather, for Geuss, a worldview is "something that characteristically and actively addresses particular people *by name*, telling them who they are and at the same time imposing on them an identity."[90] It is, according to Geuss, a boundary marker and a badge that identifies you as either in or out of the community in question. And this is the case, despite the fact that members of the same community do not necessarily "share a single determinate, well-defined, explicit set of organized beliefs about the world."[91]

This is how the figures examined here often imagine worldview can be used, but I would suggest that this is not why the idea was implemented in those communities. Rather, the deployment of worldview as a combat concept is perhaps explained by the need for communities to address their sense of siege and decline. Geuss would agree. He argues that it is

> precisely when genuine communal energies begin to dry up or when disciplinary demands are given priority over all else that the need for a "world view" in a stricter sense becomes keener. Similarly, perhaps it is those whose community is diseased,

---

90. Raymond Geuss, *Who Needs a World View?* (Cambridge, MA: Harvard University Press, 2020), 1.

91. Geuss, *Who Needs a World View?*, 38.

especially threatened, moribund, or in steep decline at the end
of a period of great vitality who need a world view.[92]

Geuss's diagnosis is suggestive. Perhaps conservative Christians, particularly evangelical and Reformed Christians, at two key junctures
in the last 150 years, felt a sense of crisis and decline and therefore
developed a self-consciousness about their diseased state. The introduction of worldview thinking was, perhaps, a response to this and
provided them with a way of explaining themselves, both to themselves and to the hostile world around them.

Conclusion

This history, and the accompanying account of the possible motivations for the emergence and deployment of worldview language in the
Christian church, should cause us to think more carefully about how
we use it today. Are Christian educators, whether teachers, lecturers,
pastors, or parents, interested in Christian worldview as a "combat
concept" in keeping with the way it was born and developed? The
answer might be yes, for some. However, for the many who answer
in the negative, the rest of this book is designed to provide a way of
taking the worldview concept in a new direction for the purposes of
education and discipleship.

The history set out in this chapter provides a cautionary tale for
Christians who want to use the old Christian worldview model in
an educational context. This model of worldview thinking was originally designed as a tool for cultural combat, but this doesn't serve
the purposes of Christian education today. We need a rethink. As a
combat concept, worldview is fundamentally a form of cultural critique, a statement about what is wrong with the world. But, as David
Lloyd Dusenbury astutely notes, critique can never be the basis of

---

92. Geuss, *Who Needs a World View?*, 39.

culture.[93] Once we have identified what is wrong, we should aim to put it right. If the broader culture is off track, should we not be aiming to course-correct and rebuild? And what else is education if not a culture-building project? We need to replace bullets with mosaic tiles—to think about building rather than shooting. As educators, we are constructing the mosaic on the ceiling of the Mausoleum of Galla Placidia, not defending it from attack. Let us leave the combat concept behind and instead think about how to create an educational masterpiece.

---

93. David Lloyd Dusenbury, *I Judge No One: A Political Life of Jesus* (London: Hurst, 2023), 4.

Chapter 3

How Do We Learn?
Education as a Building Project

When the mosaicist began work on the ceiling mosaic of the Mausoleum of Galla Placidia, he would have started by sketching out the image, first on parchment and then on the masonry. There was a master plan, even if no one could fully realize the final work of art until the last tile was laid. That plan would have been contained only in the mind of the master mosaicist. Now recall that these mosaics were likely worked on by a team of artists under the guidance of a master craftsman. If we focus our attention on the lunette of the two deer drinking from the fountain of life, that mosaic alone would have thousands of tiles, with a range of different *tesserae* types of various colors and shapes. The team of mosaicists would have worked under the watchful eye of the master to ensure they were following the plan so that the master's vision of the deer and the fountain would come to fruition.

In this chapter, I want to use the image of laying *tesserae* on a mosaic to illustrate the process of learning. When we know how people learn, we can then decide how we will proceed to teach and what we teach about. The map-making metaphor, drawn from both J. H. Bavinck and Herman Bavinck, can also work; education is the process of drawing the worldview map and unifying the intuitive data of our "worldvision" into a navigation tool for the Christian life. But for our purposes, the slow, methodical work of growing in knowledge and wisdom is more akin to the work of a mosaicist. Education, in this image, is the process of constructing a mosaic with many different tiles. It is a crafting process, with the aim of that process being a Christian worldview.

In chapters 1 and 2, I critiqued the *deductive* understanding of worldview. In contrast to the deductive understanding, my approach assumes that the Christian worldview is attained by inductive learning. Does this mean that there is no value in deductive reasoning or deductive learning? By no means. A building needs scaffolding. A person's thinking and learning needs scaffolding, too; the scaffolding of categories and frameworks within which, and around which, we build a life of reflection and learning. However, building a philosophy of Christian education around the deductive scaffolding of Christian worldview categories is a flawed exercise. We need to rethink this to make worldview work in our thinking about distinctively Christian education. The image of putting together a mosaic illustrates the idea that constructing a worldview should be an inductive process of gradually drawing the pieces together through the process of education. Worldview education should be understood *primarily* as inductive rather than deductive.

In this image, the master craftsman is not the student, nor is he any of the teachers. The master craftsman is God, the only one who has direct access to the final design, to the full picture. God is the only one who can see the *telos* of a person's education. The teacher, the parent, the pastor, and the student all work together under the guidance of God to complete the Christian worldview mosaic, tile by tile. But God is the only one who has pure and accurate knowledge of the completed mosaic.

This chapter will start us off on the journey of building a new theory of Christian worldview education. The first section will address the question of how we know what we know and will take a tour through the major theories of knowledge. The second section will narrow in on the theory of knowledge put forth by one Christian worldview thinker, Herman Bavinck, who will also be present in the third section on how we learn. With this theory of knowledge and of learning in place, we will be able in the next chapter to consider a pedagogical approach that coheres with thinking about worldview education as the process of growing in wisdom.

Different Conceptions of How We Know

Epistemology is a fundamental topic for most lines of intellectual inquiry. From the earliest philosophical writings of ancient Greece on, the problem of how we know has been at the core of the philosophical project. And every theologian worth his or her salt has to deal with the question of knowledge, the possibility of knowledge, and the acquisition of knowledge.

There have been several different approaches to the question of how we know. These approaches can be broadly separated into three categories: rationalism, empiricism, and realism. While rationalism and empiricism are insightful epistemologies, I will argue that realism offers educators a solid foundation for shaping a philosophy of Christian worldview education. Realism allows for a constructive, inductive approach to education without falling into the deductive worldview trap that plagues current worldview thinking. A key figure for realism in epistemology is the theologian Herman Bavinck. However, before proceeding to Bavinck and realism, we should consider what rationalism and empiricism have to offer us.

Rationalism is a philosophical position that asserts that the mind is the fundamental location of knowledge. The senses are deceptive, and outward appearances in the world are either imperfect or are apprehended imperfectly by our senses. This is the position argued for by the Greek philosopher Plato (c. 428–348 BC). He pointed to numerous examples of the deceptiveness of the senses; the crooked stick in the water that is actually straight, for instance.[1] The most powerful passage in his works that illustrates this is the "Allegory of

---

1. Plato, *The Republic*, 602c.

the Cave" from Book VII of his *Republic*. Indeed, the allegory comes from a long passage about the effects of education.[2] In this allegory, people are tied up in a cave staring at, and analyzing, the movement of shadows against the wall. They do this in the belief that these shadows are real things, rather than the shadows cast against the wall of the cave by a fire behind them. These people are restrained such that they cannot see the fire or the objects being paraded before it, so they remain ignorant.

One of them is set free from his bonds and sets off on a journey of discovery that starts with the realization that the shadows are merely the play of the light against real objects. The journey climaxes with an ascent out of the cave and into the world outside, lightened by the sun. In this allegory, the sun is a symbol of the truth entering the mind that enlightens the reality around the learner. Normal human experience, the experience of the detained people in the cave, is one of normal sense perception and "opinion" about things people don't know the real substance of. The enlightened mind, the one who has escaped the bonds of the deceptive world of the senses, can see things as they really are rather than as they appear. This is further explained in Plato's dialogues *Euthyphro* and *Meno*.[3] Through his mouthpiece Socrates, Plato maintains that knowledge of things is different from the knowledge of their essences. The essence of a thing, be it justice or virtue or a chair, is not clearly put forth in the examples that we see before us in this life. Rather, the philosopher needs to scale the heights of dialectical thinking to attain the true essence, the true form, of the thing in question. And that is only attainable through reason.

A second example of rationalism, one that sets in train the modern iteration of this philosophy, comes via René Descartes (1596–1650). Descartes was a doubter. He doubted everything as part of his philosophical method. And he did so to become certain. The thing that he believed was most obstructive of truth was the senses. "Whatever

---

2. Plato, *The Republic*, 514a–520a.
3. Plato, *Euthyphro*, 2a–16a; Plato, *Meno*, 70a–100b.

I have up until now accepted as most true I have acquired either from the senses or through the senses," writes Descartes.[4] But this approach to knowledge is deeply problematic because Descartes "found that the senses deceive, and it is prudent to never trust completely those who have deceived us even once."[5] So, Descartes determined to remove all prior epistemological prejudice and instead suppose that the world is controlled by an evil demon. This scenario put everything apprehended by the senses in doubt.[6] Descartes locked himself in a closet away from all deceptive appearances and concluded *cogito ergo sum*, "I think, therefore I am."[7] Or, to put it slightly differently, because I am thinking about whether I exist, I can conclude that I must exist! Notice that the *mind* is the place and foundation of truth, rather than sense perception. The mind was the only place where certainty could be found. Indeed, the mind was the foundation of certainty. This conclusion was expanded by later thinkers beyond mere epistemology to ontology (the nature of being). Under the tutelage of Hegel and his fellow "Absolute Idealists," our minds were understood as more than the seat of knowing; they were also the basis of being. Reality was understood by the Absolute Idealists to be constituted by the mind or by thought.

This emphasis on thought and mind as central to the task of knowledge was contested by the earliest Greek philosophers. Aristotle (384–322 BC), while not strictly speaking an empiricist, was not disposed to lean on the rationalist method of Plato. He argued that knowledge is readily available to us in what lies before us in the physical world. This is illustrated in his *Politics*, which begins in a different place from Plato's *Republic*. Aristotle does not begin with an ideal city, as Plato does, but starts to build a picture of political existence by

---

4. René Descartes, *Meditations on First Philosophy*, ed. John Cottingham (Cambridge: Cambridge University Press, 1996), 16.

5. Descartes, *Meditations*, 16.

6. For a simple exploration of the problem of the evil demon, see Roger Scruton, *Philosophy: Principles and Problems* (New York: Continuum, 2005), 37–42.

7. Descartes, *Meditations*, 27.

making observations about what he can see in real life. This method implies that cities that exist in our imaginations are nowhere near as useful for thinking about political life as real cities are. Aristotle pursued a more empirical approach to his study of politics, which he obviously believed would be more fruitful than the speculative rationalism exemplified by Plato.[8] Nevertheless, Aristotle's critique of rationalism was more to do with disposition and method.

It took until the early modern period to see a substantial challenge to rationalism. The empiricist movement grew as a response to Descartes, spawning contributions from many thinkers, including Francis Bacon, John Locke, and David Hume.

Francis Bacon (1561–1626) served in several capacities in the British government, but he is mostly remembered for his contributions to the development of the scientific method. In his *Novum Organon* (1620), a work simultaneously outlining how scientists ought to practice while offering a utopian vision for a scientific future, Bacon offers some initial glimpses of the kind of empiricism that was emerging.[9] "There are," asserts Bacon, "two ways to investigate and discover truth."[10] One way favors a quick ascent to general axioms and then works its way down to particulars, while the other way "elicits axioms from sense and particulars" before working up to discover general axioms.[11] Experience and experiments are of great importance in Bacon's understanding, and these are the main guides to finding out more general, higher truths. Sense experience and observation of sense data are central to Bacon's epistemological assumptions.

John Locke (1632–1704) published his major contribution to the epistemology debate in 1689 in the form of *An Essay Concerning*

---

8. Examples of this methodological divergence include: Aristotle, *Politics*, 1261a1–1261b15; *Metaphysics*, 991a; *Nicomachean Ethics*, 1096a11–1097a14.

9. Anthony Kenny, *A New History of Western Philosophy* (Oxford: Oxford University Press, 2010), 524–25.

10. Francis Bacon, *The New Organon*, ed. Lisa Jardine and Michael Silverthorne (Cambridge: Cambridge University Press, 2000), 36.

11. Bacon, *New Organon*, 36.

Human Understanding. Locke argued that any ideas that correspond with reality are real and are necessary for us to gain knowledge of the world as it is.[12] Without this correspondence between ideas and reality, we could not even think of things that exist beyond our minds.[13] Ideas themselves "give us no knowledge of real existence at all," taken on their own.[14] Indeed, according to Locke, there is no such thing as *innate ideas*, which are similar to Plato's conception of mathematical truths that exist in the mind prior to birth. Not even knowledge of God's existence is something innate to humans; it must be attained by "sense, perception, and reason."[15] Locke affirms that we can have genuine knowledge of ourselves and God. He is not a skeptic. But he also argued that the "knowledge of the existence of any other thing" can be attained "only by sensation." Sense experience is the way to knowing things other than God or ourselves, according to Locke.[16]

One of the leading lights of the Scottish Enlightenment was the empiricist David Hume (1711–1776), famous for, among many things, his historical writing as well as his religious skepticism. Hume's *Enquiry Concerning Human Understanding* (1748) has become a classic, in part because the Prussian philosopher Immanuel Kant (1724–1804) said that Hume's empiricism awoke him from his "dogmatic slumbers."[17] Hume took the question of cause and effect as basic in his argument about the nature of human knowledge in the *Enquiry*, and asserted that "the knowledge of this relation [of cause and effect] is not, in any instance, attained by reasonings *a priori*; but arises

---

12. John Locke, *An Essay Concerning Human Understanding*, ed. John Yolton (London: Dent, 1978), 314–17 (II.XXX).

13. Martha Brandt Bolton, "The Taxonomy of Ideas in Locke's *Essay*," in *The Cambridge Companion to Locke's "Essay Concerning Human Understanding*," ed. Lex Newman (Cambridge: Cambridge University Press, 2007), 94.

14. Locke, *Essay*, 217 (IV.IX.1).

15. Locke, *Essay*, 218 (IV.X.1).

16. Kenny, *History of Western Philosophy*, 540; Roger Scruton, *A Short History of Modern Philosophy: From Descartes to Wittgenstein* (London: Routledge, 2001), 82.

17. Roger Scruton, *Kant: A Very Short Introduction* (Oxford: Oxford University Press, 2001), 25.

entirely from experience."[18] Further, the operations of "all the laws of nature, and all the operations of bodies without exception, are known only by experience."[19] Deploying a famous illustration of billiard balls knocking against one another, Hume asserted that there are no grounds whatsoever for presuming that humans know anything inherent about any objects. Inferences about operations of bodies in the world are drawn only from custom rather than objective reason.[20] The only way we can know anything about anything is if we observe the thing with our senses.

Herman Bavinck's Realism

So where does this leave us in relation to knowledge? Relying on reason, on ideas alone, for knowledge of reality is not a stable foundation because there must be something that reason attaches itself to in the real world. The gap between the knower and thing being known is too large in a rationalist framework, and the empiricists are right to argue that taking reason as the supreme ground of knowledge is problematic. However, a similar critique could be turned on empiricism. The gap between the knower and known is too large, and people must have a preconceived rational framework of some kind that orders our interpretation of sense experience. If reason cannot be relied on as the foundation of knowledge, and neither can sense experience, where should we turn?[21] One thinker who deploys the worldview motif *and* critiques these epistemologies is Herman Bavinck.

---

18. David Hume, *An Enquiry Concerning Human Understanding*, ed. Tom L. Beauchamp (Oxford: Oxford University Press, 2000), 25 (4.1.6).

19. Hume, *Enquiry*, 26 (4.1.9).

20. Hume, *Enquiry*, 26 (4.1.8); Kenny, *History of Western Philosophy*, 563–65.

21. The rationalist and empiricist attempts to explain the basis of knowledge were brilliantly mediated by Immanuel Kant, who synthesized the role of reason and experience into his theory of transcendental idealism. A helpful introduction to this is in Scruton, *Kant*, 16–31. For the purposes of this discussion, we will leave Kant aside. This is not a work on the history of philosophy, and I cannot deal with this extremely interesting and important aspect of the history of ideas here. Suffice to say that Kant's theory ultimately falls foul of the same critiques levelled at rationalism. See *RD* 1:215–17.

Like Kuyper, Bavinck was a leader in the Dutch Neo-Calvinist movement. Born in 1854 in Holland into an ecclesiastical household, Bavinck followed in his father's footsteps and became a minister in the Christian Reformed Church. His talents lay in academic theology, though, and he pursued a doctorate before becoming a professor at the Theological School at Kampen. He joined Kuyper as a leader in the Anti-Revolutionary Party and also joined the faculty of the Free University in the early twentieth century, writing numerous important and influential works on theology, ethics, and culture. By the time he died in 1921 he was both a professor and a member of the Dutch Senate, and his legacy and influence continue to grow.[22]

Bavinck offers an alternative approach to worldview thinking by applying an inductive method to the process of acquiring knowledge, even if he did so imperfectly and inconsistently. His epistemology allows us to think about learning and worldview construction inductively. In this aspect of his thought, Bavinck stands in contrast with Abraham Kuyper. Kuyper started from above and worked down, but Bavinck did the reverse.[23] Kuyper would assume a high-level vantage point, whereas Bavinck assumed a starting point. Bavinck was not consistent in his approach to inductive worldview thinking, and I won't adopt his worldview philosophy *in toto*. His thinking points us in the right direction, though, especially his epistemology. His approach to the question of how we know provides us with a coherent framework by which we can map the constructive worldview education project.

Bavinck's core "worldview" text has the unsurprising title *Christian Worldview*. The ideas contained in it were first aired as a rectorial address at the Free University of Amsterdam in 1904, with the initial edition of the book appearing later that year.[24] According to N.

---

22. There are two biographies in English of Bavinck: James Eglinton, *Bavinck: A Critical Biography* (Grand Rapids: Baker Academic, 2020), and Ron Gleason, *Herman Bavinck: Pastor, Churchman, Statesman, and Theologian* (Phillipsburg, NJ: P&R, 2010).

23. Eglinton, *Bavinck: A Critical Biography*, 181–82.

24. Herman Bavinck, *Christelijke werelbeschouwing* (Kampen: Bos, 1904).

Gray Sutanto, Bavinck's overall argument is that "intellectual unity depends upon recognizing the resources that the Christian faith possesses for academic pursuit."[25] There is, according to Bavinck, "a disharmony between our thinking and feeling, between our willing and acting."[26] This points to the lack of a "unified world-and-life view" in the modern world.[27] Christianity is the key unifying factor, according to Bavinck, as the "Christian faith" is the "foundation and cornerstone of all knowledge and science."[28] It seems that Bavinck is claiming that in order to truly know, you need to be a Christian.[29]

This implication of Bavinck's thought is made explicit in the writings of Abraham Kuyper, who argued that there are two kinds of "science" (by which he means knowledge).[30] For Kuyper and, it seems, for Bavinck, our knowledge of reality is determined by our starting point. And not just any starting point. Kuyper's framework posits religious convictions as the basis of our approach to science and scholarship. This understanding of the connection between religious belief and knowledge is linked to the deductive worldview approach, which assumes big-picture tenets, especially religious beliefs, are fundamental to learning and the study of the world. This idea has an intuitive appeal, especially to people who are seeking to differentiate a particularly Christian approach to education from other approaches. But there are problems with it.

---

25. Nathaniel Gray Sutanto, *God and Knowledge* (London: T&T Clark, 2020), 50.

26. *CW*, 22.

27. *CW*, 22.

28. *CW*, 39.

29. Sutanto, *God and Knowledge*, 45–50. Cf. the helpful essay on presuppositionalist critiques of Bavinck's epistemology by Laurence O'Donnell, "'Bavinck's Bug' or 'Van Tillian' Hypochondria?: An Analysis of Prof. Oliphint's Assertion that Cognitive Realism and Reformed Theology Are Incompatible," in *For the Healing of the Nations: Essays on Creation, Redemption, and Neo-Calvinism*, ed. Peter Escalante and W. Bradford Littlejohn (Charleston: Davenant, 2014), 139–72.

30. Abraham Kuyper, *Principles of Sacred Theology*, trans. J. Hendrik de Vries (Grand Rapids: Eerdmans, 1954), 150. Cf. Nicholas Wolterstorff, *Educating for Shalom: Essays on Christian Higher Education*, ed. Clarence W. Joldersma and Gloria Goris Stronks (Grand Rapids: Eerdmans, 2004), 221–25.

First, the assertion that knowledge of the world depends on a unifying overarching religious belief does not help us make sense of the educational project.[31] Nor is it true. Christians and non-Christians do not have a different epistemological status when it comes to the sciences and scholarship. Nor is a Christian closer to the truth than a non-Christian in the study of any subject, other than theology and ethics. In theology, as Bavinck rightly argues, the piety of the theologian has a substantial impact on their work.[32] This doesn't mean there is no such thing as a Christian worldview. There can be a Christian worldview without the elements of that view becoming necessary for true access to knowledge. Indeed, it is my view that Christian educators can faithfully and confidently fulfill their calling in educating Christians and non-Christians, and in either case, they can be helping their students move toward a Christian worldview. That issue aside, we can now look closely at Bavinck's realist epistemology to assist us in thinking about knowing and learning.[33]

Bavinck starts his discussion of epistemology by critiquing the two positions I have unpacked above. The basis of his critique is the assertion that both empiricism and rationalism assume a disharmony between subject and object. Bavinck asserts that reality points to the existence of harmony between these two. The categories of subject and object might seem to add unnecessary philosophical complexity to this discussion, but they are easy to grasp. The subject is the person doing the thinking and perceiving. The object is the thing being thought about and perceived. You are the subject, and this page is the object. The letters you are reading are also an object. And the

---

31. Cf. Bavinck's comments at *RD*, 1:110.

32. *RD*, 1:91. This is not to suggest that there isn't any kind of intellectual dependence on Christianity at all, in terms of knowing the truth about things outside of theology. I understand the impact of Christian faith on knowledge to be on a spectrum, and that spectrum is not consistently applied to all individual people. The best explanation I have come across is in Emil Brunner, *Revelation and Reason: The Christian Doctrine of Faith and Knowledge*, trans. Olive Wyon (London: SCM Press, 1947), 374–96.

33. For a thorough discussion on Bavinck's view of the Christian's epistemological status with regard to the sciences, see Sutanto, *God and Knowledge*, 56–68.

hand you are holding the book with is an object in relation to your-self as the knowing, thinking subject. And Bavinck believes that any coherent account of the world requires a "harmony between subject and object, and between knowing and being."[34] The knower and the thing being known must be in proper relation. Any project of gaining knowledge, any kind of science, "always consists in a logical relation between subject and object," such that "our view of science depends on the way we relate the two."[35] We must find a way to resolve this problem of the relationship between the knower and the thing being known, and Bavinck does not believe either empiricism or rational-ism helps with this.

Empiricism falls down, according to Bavinck, at a number of points. The first is that it is not merely the bodily organs that per-ceive, but actual people. "It is not the eye that sees or the ear that hears but the person himself who sees through the eye that sees or the ear that hears."[36] In other words, empiricism fails to account for the existence of a human consciousness, or soul, that is active in the perceiving of the world. Our minds are not a mere blank slate (or *tabula rasa*). Rather, it is "the person himself who perceives and con-nects, compares and judges, the perceptions" that our senses take in.[37] People are not vacant receptors of sense information but, to use an information technology metaphor, come pre-loaded with applications and data.[38] They are "a totality of life from the very first moment of [their] existence."[39] Empiricism also fails to make sense of the fact that people don't merely possess "particular and incidental truths"; they also necessarily possess "universal ... truths" that provide some kind

---

34. *CW*, 32.

35. *RD*, 1:214.

36. *RD*, 1:220.

37. *RD*, 1:220.

38. Herman Bavinck, *Philosophy of Revelation: A New Annotated Edition*, trans. Cory Brock and Nathaniel Gray Sutanto (Peabody: MA: Hendrickson, 2018), 56, hereafter abbreviated as *PoR*.

39. *PoR*, 55.

of unity to the particular.[40] The thinker, the scientist, the philosopher, always brings values, preconceived ideas, and universals to the table when taking on new information. Empiricism is, therefore, a dead end.

Rationalism suffers the same fate, according to Bavinck. This is because, with both empiricism and rationalism, "a correspondence between thinking and being ... is lost."[41] Rationalism, and the resulting idealism, is "contrary to all experience."[42] People naturally and automatically ascribe "objectivity and independent reality to the things perceived."[43] We also naturally distinguish between internal thoughts and external objects when we consider the world and its relationship to our ideas. Putting our subjective experience aside, Bavinck also points to the impossibility of thought grasping and producing being (or things) apart from being itself.[44] "We have to make a choice," argues Bavinck. Either "the perceptions we gain by way of the senses are all subjective, or they correspond to an objective reality."[45] We cannot sustain an account of the world and our knowledge of it with rationalism and idealism. Somehow, sense perception must be joined to our ideas, and it cannot be through the explanation offered by idealism. Our minds do not cause our sense perceptions, and our senses are not the only receptors. Our souls are also involved in apprehending and interpreting what the senses perceive.

Bavinck notes that both rationalism and empiricism fail at the same point. With both theories of knowledge, "the concept of truth ... a correspondence between thinking and being, is lost."[46] For us to believe the truth really is out there, we must hold to an epistemology that is neither empiricism nor rationalism. The gap between our minds and the world must be overcome. This is because real

---

40. RD, 1:220.
41. CW, 33.
42. RD, 1:217.
43. RD 1:217.
44. RD, 1:218.
45. RD, 1:218.
46. CW, 31.

knowledge requires there to be real relationship. "Knowing is always
... a relation between subject and object [such that as] soon one or
both falls away, there is no more knowing."[47] Furthermore, "knowledge of truth is possible only if we begin with the fact that subject
and object, and knowing and being, correspond to each other."[48] The
very foundations of scholarship, intellectual investigation, and science,
rest on this being true.

The solution is to start with ordinary experience and to assume
that there is unity between what we see and what we know. The
world and the organs that perceive that world and interpret it have a
"common origin," according to Bavinck.[49] The origin is God, the creator of our senses and brain. This God is also the creator of the world
that is apprehended by those organs. So, too, our souls are created by
the God who made the world that the soul interacts with through the
senses. Therefore, the assumption that we are to base our theory of
knowledge on is "the universal and natural certainty of human beings
concerning the objectivity and truth of their knowledge."[50] This is the
normal way that humans live. We assume that what we are seeing
is there, and then we think about what we see. All the way through
this process, we assume that our perceptions and apprehension of
the things are reliable. We accept that the world exists. We presume
that what we see is *really there*. As Bavinck puts it, we must assume
that the world and the representation of that world mediated by our
senses and interpreted in our own minds are basically in correspondence. "We do not know," according to Bavinck, "how the world
can exist, or how in this world consciousness is possible, yet no one
doubts the reality of either."[51] These facts about our experience of

---

47. *CW*, 34.
48. *CW*, 38.
49. *CW*, 38–39.
50. *RD*, 1:223.
51. *PoR*, 59.

the world and of our apprehension of it mean it makes sense to start with everyday experience and sense perception.[52]

This acceptance that the external world that we sense and move in is as it appears matches what we see in the Bible. The Scriptures point us to God's revelation in his creation. This is in contrast to the claims of rationalism, which says we should start with our reason. Rather, the starting point ought to be our experience and sense of the world.[53] Romans 1:19–20 is a good example: "For what can be known about God is plain to them, because God has shown it to them. For his invisible attributes ... have been clearly perceived, ever since the creation of the world, in the things that have been made." The apostle Paul, here, affirms that knowledge (about God, no less!) can be garnered through sense perception and observation of things that were created by God. The psalms speak repeatedly about the fruits of observing God's general revelation. Psalm 8:3–4:

> When I look at the heavens, the work of your fingers,
>   the moon and the stars, which you have set in place,
> what is man that you are mindful of him,
>   and the son of man that you care for him?

Psalm 19 points the reader to the work of God in the heavens, observable with the senses. Psalm 34:8 calls us to "taste and see that the LORD is good!" Psalm 46:8 urges us to "behold the works of the LORD." Psalm 66:5 says, "Come and see what God has done." Solomon prompts his son to "Go to the ant ... consider her ways, and be wise" (Prov 6:6) God speaks to Job "out of the whirlwind" (Job 38:1) and refers Job to his knowledge of the creation across dozens of verses. "Behold, Behemoth," says God, "which I made as I made you" (Job 40:15). The Bible does not call our perception of created reality into question, but rather affirms it. So, while our sense perceptions can be faulty (as Plato and Descartes would argue), they nevertheless offer

---

52. *CW*, 39.
53. *CW*, 39.

us the surest knowledge of reality.[54] As Thomas Aquinas argues, our souls gain knowledge of reality outside of us by way of the senses.[55]

It would seem, then, that Bavinck is siding with the empiricists in arguing that we can only trust our senses. But Bavinck wants to bring sense and reason together in a single theory of epistemology that is neither empiricist nor rationalist. "None of this," he says, "denies that the object can only be known by the subject and be known through thinking."[56] He brings reason and sense perception together by adopting a theory of universals that organizes the particulars that our senses bring in. According to Bavinck, "There exists a certainty other than [the] scientific demonstrative certainty" that sense perception offers. We can be certain that there are universal truths that are not demonstrable by scientific investigation. "Experience," writes Bavinck, "only teaches us that something is, but not that it has to be." How do we get these universal truths? Bavinck argues that our intellect is "activated" by the sensible world and then moves to organize what it perceives. The intellect has the "power," the "ability," the "inclination," and the "fitness," to form ideas about the world that "precede all reasoning and proof."[57]

So, while we can immediately grasp that a class of students is greater than a single student, and while we can immediately know that we shouldn't thrust our colleague's hand into a fire, it is a different level of thought to organize these bits of knowledge according to higher truths. The class might be greater than the single student, but we also recognize that the single student is of infinite value because of her image-bearing status. We know that shoving someone's hand into the fire is hazardous for them (and for you!), but we also recognize that doing so would not simply burn flesh; it would also be manifestly evil and malicious. "Every human, even the most simple,

---

54. CW, 37.

55. Thomas Aquinas, Summa Theologiae, Question 84, Article 6.

56. CW, 35.

57. RD, 1:224–25.

applies these basic concepts and principles in life without any scientific reflection ... and with the utmost certainty."[58] We just know that grievously injuring someone is evil, and we just know that the single student really matters even in light of the larger class.

This intuitive knowledge of universal principles, like the principles of morality, is part of what Bavinck characterizes as a Christian realism that "maintains both the freedom and the constraints of the human mind."[59] We can raise ourselves up to the realm of universal principles, but we must prioritize connection with reality. Christian realism embraces both the ideal and the real. We can be confident that what we observe with our senses, what Bavinck calls "representations," are true apprehensions of reality. At the same time, we must move from representation to scientific knowledge. We must seek the universal that emerges from our apprehension of the particular facts. We must reach for higher-level concepts that help us organize what our senses apprehend.[60] This is a process Bavinck characterizes as acquiring scientific knowledge; this is the task of scholarship and learning.

We can summarize the above by asserting some principles of scientific activity. The first is that God is the basis, and the first principle, of being. Everything that exists does so because God thought of it and made it by his word.[61] Theologians sometimes use the word *archetypal* to refer to God's firsthand knowledge of himself, and we might use the same word in relation to God's firsthand knowledge of his creation. What humans learn about the world God made is called *ectypal* knowledge. This is a knowledge of things contained in the divine mind, but it is secondhand. As Bavinck puts it, God gives this knowledge to "the human mind in the works of his hands."[62] This knowledge of reality is not the same as God's in its perfection or

---

58. *RD*, 1:226.
59. *RD*, 1:226.
60. *CW*, 50.
61. This entire paragraph is reliant on *RD*, 1:233.
62. *RD*, 1:233; *CW*, 46–48.

comprehensiveness. Indeed, this ectypal knowledge is severely limited! We are, in my view, groping around in the dark with a lighted match when it comes to knowing all there is to know about creation. We can see enough and can grow in our understanding of reality, but we are constrained by sin and our status as creatures. Nevertheless, we can simultaneously affirm that it is possible to have ectypal knowledge and that this knowledge is limited. We get this limited knowledge through what Bavinck calls "the external foundation for all science."[63] That is, we gain knowledge through apprehension of the stuff of creation. Creation speaks truth to us just by being there. Finally, God passes an internal knowledge on to us by way of what is known as the "light of reason."[64] Human reason ascertains truth in the mind through the apprehension of created reality. This is the external connecting to the internal. Put another way, this is the uniting of subject (the thinker or knower) and object (reality or the thing being known).

The Christian realism that Bavinck presents offers an attractive path toward a theory of learning. We can be confident that our senses provide a ground for knowledge of the world as it really is, despite our limitations. We can also be confident that our desire for unity of knowledge about the world is grounded in a natural drive toward higher scientific knowledge. Both reason and sense perception have their place, both subject and object are connected. And they are primarily connected through the fact that the Triune God created them all with the intention that they meet in harmonious relationship through the process of learning.

Growing in Knowledge, or How We Learn

The question of how people learn is a complex one, but it is made substantially less complex if we affirm a Bavinckian-style realism. Trusting our senses and our capacity to organize what our senses bring to our attention provides grounds on which we can confidently

---

63. RD, 1:233.
64. RD, 1:233.

describe how we learn. I want to sketch a theory of learning in this section so that we can fit it into the broader understanding of the Christian worldview education project. This is not intended to be a definitive word on pedagogy or theories of learning. I concede that humans are far more complex than any single theory allows for. What I offer here is a theoretical foundation for understanding Christian education as a worldview-building endeavor that avoids the pitfalls of the typical deductive approach to worldview.

A person's worldview is not given but is constructed through education, and worldview education is a team construction project. This framing of worldviews as constructed rather than given needs a significant qualification, though, as there is always a master plan to which the individual worldview corresponds. I expand on this more below. Earlier, I also described the educational process as a constructive project similar to the creation of a mosaic. Mosaicists gradually build a beautiful work of art, *tessera* by *tessera*, tile by tile, piece by piece. The mosaic is akin to the finished product of the educational process, and for our purposes that finished product is a Christian view of the world. No one has the master plan of this finished product apart from God. And even then, God's archetypal knowledge of reality is necessarily superior to and different from our limited and flawed ectypal knowledge. Nevertheless, I want to work with this metaphor of education as a supervised construction project akin to the team-creation of a mosaic. To that end, I will now explore how people learn.

Let us start with the claim I made above differentiating inductive and deductive approaches to worldview thinking. We don't generally start a learning process with a completed, big picture of reality and then fit everything we learn into that picture. We start with what the *other* Bavinck, J. H. Bavinck (Herman's nephew), calls a "worldvision," which is an intuitive, subjective grasp of the world that lacks the unifying elements of a worldview.[65] The process of acquiring knowledge generally requires people to move from particular to universal, rather

---

65. *PW*, 30.

than the other way around. Deductive categories, which are how we organize our apprehension of universal reality, are crucial for teaching and learning. A good example for Christians are the truths taught in the Bible about God and his relationship to the world.

In general, then, we learn by moving from the particular to the universal. I argued above that people are perfectly capable of doing this. In many cases, it is a simple and automatic process. But in some cases, it is difficult and, even if it isn't, the process needs refinement. Often our apprehension of universal categories and truths, the way we organize our knowledge of particulars and situate our "worldvision," is imprecise. Plato is sometimes proven right: our senses do deceive, just as our heart does (Jer 17:9). Education is one way of increasing our capacity to organize what we garner via sense experience *and* improve that organization. The fact that we typically gain knowledge by moving from smaller pieces of truth to the larger picture implies that we need to learn inductively; that is, we need to take the sense data that we acquire and grow our understanding of it.

So where do we begin in framing a theory of learning? There are several existing learning frameworks, theories of how we learn, that can help us. The first is directly related to Bavinck's realism. Realists affirm two important things. First, realism affirms that there is a meaningful order to the world. Whether that order is described in terms of a "natural law," a creation order, or whatever, the basic idea is that reality is an ordered and meaningful whole. Everything in that reality either behaves according to the given order or else it exhibits qualities that show exceptions to that order that are observable and perspicuous. The exceptions and their perspicacity prove the existence of the overall order. A realist account of reality also affirms that the particular aspects of reality, the things in the world, are connected to that overall order. These particulars are part of a logical whole and in themselves exhibit qualities that are related to that higher order. For example, a particular tree is really a tree, not just because you or God call it that but because there is a higher conceptual frame that the tree fits into that is meaningful. Trees really are trees, and we can think about them as such. In other words, the realist affirms that the transcendent ordering of reality is organically connected to the temporal, observable order.[66]

Bavinck puts it like this: "All things are brought forth from the wisdom of the Word of God," and therefore "all things exist according to 'reason.' "[67] This reason is not the abstract, blind "spirit" of Hegel's absolute or any other kind of blind transcendent force. Rather, Bavinck understands reality as knowable because of God's "foreknowledge" of reality. This foreknowledge is not that of Romans 8:29 ("For those whom he foreknew he also predestined ..."), which is foreknowing related to what theologians call the *ordo salutis* (order of salvation). Rather, Bavinck is positing that reality is a "manifestation" of God's mind. Reality existed in the mind of God first (hence, foreknowledge) and then was manifested as reality for us to know.[68] Based on this, Bavinck asserts that created reality comes to us "along the path of sense perception, then through the thinking activity of the 'mind,' " before it takes on the properties of knowledge within our minds.[69]

This realist philosophical framework has implications for learning and education. With the realist, we can affirm that the world out there contains lots of little pieces of truth that we really can make sense of. People observe the world around them and gradually refine their understanding. In their spiritual lives, people of faith renew their minds spiritually through reading the Scriptures and prayer. People who are learning and growing in their knowledge notice connections between different pieces of reality and see patterns in the way different aspects of the world relate. And gradually they build a picture of the world as it really is. People gather bits of that truth

---

66. On the ancient picture of the cosmos as an ordered and meaningful reality, see Remi Brague, *The Wisdom of the World* (Chicago: University of Chicago Press, 2003); *PoR*, 50.

67. *CW*, 45.

68. *CW*, 45.

69. *CW*, 46.

and organize them into categories.[70] People learn inductively. This, it seems to me, is the way people grow in their knowledge of reality. To quote Aristotle, we become "familiar with the primitives [i.e., first principles] by induction."[71] Sense perception and the data that it offers are the basis upon which we build up universal categories of organizing things in the world. We can affirm with the empiricist that our senses provide the first step in our understanding of reality, but we should affirm the rationalist's point that we can apply our reason to the organization of this sense data because there really is an ordered whole to fit that data into.

This is an optimistic place to start if you are an educator. The world that you are teaching about makes sense, even when there is ambiguity and confusion about it (which there often is!). This realist understanding is also a meaningful place to start if you are a Christian educator. It means that you and your students are working on a big, beautiful project that is designed by a Master artist. Despite our severely limited capacity to know about reality, all the elements of that reality explored in your teaching are useful and fit into a whole that is given and meaningful.

To briefly return to the mosaic metaphor, the master plan of the mosaic is set in place by a loving, reasonable God who has created an ordered reality that you and your students can learn about with the confidence that what you are observing corresponds with that reality. All the tiles of the mosaic fit into something big and meaningful.[72] Of course, as Christians, we know that the fall impacts our intellects. We need to accept that we all make mistakes and don't always have a perfect grasp of reality. Francis Bacon was right to point out how easily

---

70. George R. Knight, *Philosophy of Education: An Introduction in Christian Perspective* (Berrien Springs, MI: Andrews University Press, 2006), 50–54.

71. Aristotle, *Posterior Analytics*, II:19; translation from Aristotle, *The Complete Works of Aristotle: The Revised Oxford Translation, One-Volume Digital Edition*, ed. Jonathan Barnes (Princeton: Princeton University Press, 2014), 375; James Bowen and Peter R. Hobson, *Theories of Education: Studies in Significant Innovation in Western Educational Thought*, 2nd ed. (New York: John Wiley & Sons,1987), 80–90.

72. Cf. *PoR*, 67.

our interpretation of reality can be distorted by unhelpful biases and filters, which he calls "idols of the mind."[73] Despite this, Christian realism affirms that efforts to apprehend reality will, over time and with refinement, work toward truth.[74]

The master plan of the mosaic is set in place by God, who is the one who made all and knows all. God has also made much of created reality knowable. Therefore, educators and students ought to see education as the process of constructing this worldview mosaic according to God's master plan, which is the overarching order of reality. While there is a construction project occurring, it is not one founded on the subjective apprehension of sense data. Rather, I want to frame education as the deliberate, methodical enhancement of the natural inclination that people have to grow in their understanding of given reality. Put another way, education is the way people accelerate their ability to make intelligent and informed connections between things in the world, between things in the world and themselves, and between things and God. These connections could be construed as relations, and therefore education could be framed as being about those relations.

This idea about education being fundamentally about relations was put forth by the educator and philosopher Charlotte Mason (1842–1923). In her book *School Education* (1905), Mason described education as the way to a student having a full life. (We might use the word "fulfilling" instead of "full.") "Every child is heir to an enormous patrimony, heir to all the ages, inheritor of all the present," writes Mason.[75] "The question is what are the formalities ... necessary to put him in possession of that which is his?"[76] Mason was writing about the education of children, but the same question could be asked about educating adults. How can we help people, be they children or adults,

---

73. Bacon, *New Organon*, 46–53.

74. *CW*, 36–37.

75. Charlotte M. Mason, *School Education* (London: Kegan Paul, Trench, Trubner, 1905). Edition cited here: Charlotte Mason, *School Education* (Jilliby: Living Book Press, 2017), 186.

76. Mason, *School Education*, 186.

connect with reality in a meaningful and true way? This ought to be the goal of education, and it seems to me that Mason had a helpful way of framing this when she called education "the Science of Relations."[77]

This idea of "relations" links well with Bavinck's realism. Bavinck says that all "cognition consists in a peculiar *relation* of subject and object."[78] All thinking about reality is about relations between the thinker and the objects of thought. I would add to this that we also think about the relations between different objects. According to Mason, we all "personally have relations with all that there is in the present, all that there has been in the past, and all that there will be in the future—with all above us and all about us."[79] Having a fulfilling life "depend[s] upon how far we apprehend these relationships and how many of them we lay hold of."[80] As people, we relate to everything else. We have a relationship with other people, but also other things. You have a particular relation to your chair, for instance. And you have a relation to this book. You have a relation to your neighbor's hamster, and to the koala in the zoo, and to the sea. Indeed, your world and your experience of the world are constituted by a complex, innumerable series of relations. You also have relations with other people, and with God. There are, then, three kinds of relations for every person: relations with the world, with other people, and with God.

If education is the science of relations, as Mason suggests, then the job of the educator is to help the student "apprehend these relationships." Education is the process of learning about other things and other people, past, present, and future. The purpose of education is to facilitate the student's relationship to these things so the student can live well in the world. We will return to this concept of living well in the world as an outcome of education in the following chapters when I bring in the concept of wisdom. Indeed, Mason uses the

---

77. Mason, *School Education*, 185.
78. *PoR*, 66. Emphasis added.
79. Mason, *School Education*, 185–86.
80. Mason, *School Education*, 186.

same concept to describe education when she calls it "applied wisdom."[81] But for now, I want to synthesize this concept of education as the science of relations with the realist epistemology and inductive understanding of learning that goes along with that epistemology. In short, I want to frame the task of education with these conceptions of learning that we have just explored.

Conclusion

In this chapter, we have explored the related questions of how we know and how we learn. The goal of this process was to find a way of thinking about knowing and learning that would help us frame Christian worldview education. Rather than thinking of worldview education as a deductive project, whereby we start with a high-level view of reality and then deduce the details, we ought to think of it as an inductive project. To use the metaphor of the creation of the ceiling mosaics of the Mausoleum of Galla Placidia, rather than teachers and students starting with the master mosaicist's plan, we ought to start with the tiles and build from there. We are mere laborers on the mosaic. We have no say over the final design, and we also have very limited knowledge of that design. We are not God, and what we know is only a dim relation to God's knowledge of reality. Nevertheless, we can affirm that reality as God has made it is, in principle, knowable. So we can discern where some of the tiles go on the mosaic. A Christian worldview education is like the construction of a mosaic, with the goal being a beautiful image of reality as God has created it.

How can we frame knowing and learning within this kind of understanding of the worldview education project? I suggest that we embrace the epistemology of realism, with a model realist being the worldview theologian Herman Bavinck. Bavinckian realism affirms the existence of objective, created reality and affirms that this reality generally corresponds with our sense perception of it. Not only this, but Bavinck's framework offers us a way to bring together the

---

81. Mason, *School Education*, 75.

elements of the mosaic masterplan and the subjective and constructive aspects of education. As educators and students, we are reaching for a particular vision of reality that we know exists, and which we see glimpses of. Yet our experience doesn't give us the master plan. Indeed, our apprehension of that plan is extremely limited.

So, we use our sense experience to construct an understanding of reality, one that we believe corresponds (however imperfectly) with the overarching, meaningful design of that reality. We expand and refine our understanding of reality through learning. Following Charlotte Mason's framing of education as "the science of relations," we can see that the education process is one of apprehending and building proper relations between the learner and the world, between the learner and God. As relations are properly understood and applied with wisdom, we see different tiles being placed in the worldview mosaic and, subsequently, there ought to be greater correspondence between the worldview mosaic and God's masterplan.

As I conclude this chapter, I want to anticipate an idea that I will flesh out in more detail in chapter 5. That is, a Christian worldview is a true unity of the subjective mind and the objective world, and this unity is grounded in the Christian confession. This worldview necessarily remains subjective and limited because we don't have God's view of reality, and I earlier argued that we ought to reject the notion that Christians have a special epistemic status over non-Christians. However, I also want to affirm that in the theories of knowledge and learning outlined above, we can affirm with Bavinck that God is the ground of all knowledge.[82] Subject and object, knowledge and reality, all correspond because reality is an expression of the divine mind. As Bavinck puts it, "we know things because they are, but they are because God has known them."[83] This means that, in the end, human

---

82. As Sutanto summarizes, "Ontologically, divine wisdom continues to sustain science whether one accepts [God] or not. One *undermines* one's justification for believing in the pursuit of science ... when one denies [God's] wisdom." Sutanto, *God and Knowledge*, 68.

83. *CW*, 46.

thought must seek after the higher truth about the Creator, because all knowledge finds its unity and knowledge in Him.

Echoing John 1, Bavinck writes that "all truth is understood in the Wisdom ... who was in the beginning with God and who himself was God."[84] The Wisdom referred to here is Jesus Christ, the eternally begotten Son, the second person of the Trinity. What is the connection of this Wisdom, which is expressed in the created world, with the wisdom that we seek? I would say that wisdom is the content and the aim of a Christian education, and that the building of a Christian worldview requires the acquisition of wisdom. Wisdom, according to Bavinck, "seeks for the final grounds of all things and builds a worldview thereupon."[85] This building project, and the parts of that project that make up the Christian worldview mosaic, will be worked out in the next chapter as we consider the topic of wisdom.

---

84. *CW*, 47.
85. *CW*, 50.

Chapter 4

What About Sophia? Education as Growing in Wisdom

The *tesserae* that coalesce in the lunette mosaic depicting the deer in the Mausoleum of Galla Placidia are made of a variety of materials. Mosaicists could call on a range of tile materials, such as marble, limestone, terracotta, beycoz stone, and glass.[1] Each type of material would offer different colors, hues, reflective and shimmering effects, and texture to the mosaic images. These *tesserae* were individually extracted from larger pieces of rock or, in the case of glass *tesserae*, were manufactured in glass workshops in Europe and the Middle East. The process of creating each *tessera* may have been extremely time-consuming, but ultimately each tile could contribute to an amazing work of sacred art.

These mosaics were not intended to be a final and definitive picture of reality. There was no pretension in the minds of the early Christian mosaicists that they could comprehensively and accurately represent such a thing by their art. Rather, they were aiming to transport the worshiper who was in the church or chapel from one understanding of reality to another. The person who came into the Mausoleum of Galla Placidia was meant to move from a gritty

---

1. The mosaic of Archangel Gabriel in the Hagia Sophia in Istanbul has these materials, and is discussed in Liz James, *Mosaics in the Medieval World: From Late Antiquity to the Fifteenth Century* (Cambridge: Cambridge University Press, 2017), 23.

reality outside the chapel to a cosmic vision inside, dominated by the kingship of Christ and the final destiny of humanity.

Like a mosaic, Christian worldview is not meant to give a definitive picture of reality. But the big question I have left unanswered thus far is this: What are the tiles of the Christian worldview mosaic made up of? What is the material from which the *tesserae* of the worldview mosaic is constructed? The answer I offer in this chapter is *wisdom*. Each tile is a piece of wisdom, and a Christian education is the process of placing wisdom tiles on the worldview mosaic. Christian worldview education can be understood not as an attempt to perfect someone's scientific understanding but as the process of helping students think and act in accordance with the wisdom of God. I asked in the last chapter how a student might come to get these tiles, and the answer was: gradually, piece by piece. In this chapter, I want to explore the biblical concept of wisdom, the way wisdom is taught in the Bible, and the way that wisdom makes up the pieces of the worldview mosaic.

There are lots of imperatives in the Bible. "Be fruitful and multiply and fill the earth" (Gen 1:28) is a creation, or cultural, mandate, applying to all the people and families of humanity. "Go therefore and make disciples of all nations" (Matt 28:19) is a command spoken by Jesus to his disciples, the opening of what is known as the Great Commission, a task assigned to the church. One commonly overlooked imperative in Scripture is found in Proverbs 4:7: "Get wisdom!" Benjamin T. Quinn suggests that this imperative "bears as much weight as the better-known imperatives from Scripture."[2] I agree. It is addressed to all readers and is delivered in a pedagogical setting. The origin of the text is the king's court, as evidenced by the Solomonic authorship (Prov 1:1), but the teaching occurs in the home and comes through the parents (Prov 1:8, 4:1–9).[3] The father speaks to his son, giving him, in Derek Kidner's

---

2. Benjamin T. Quinn, *Walking in God's Wisdom: The Book of Proverbs* (Bellingham, WA: Lexham, 2018), 2.

3. Bruce K. Waltke, *The Book of Proverbs: Chapters 1–15* (Grand Rapids: Eerdmans, 2004), 62–63.

words, "a course of education in the life of wisdom."[4] The book of
Proverbs provides us with a biblical vision of education, where the
teacher (the father) implores his student (the son) to seek a life of
wisdom. This is what a Christian worldview education is about.

Wisdom Defined

Two significant traditions influence how we understand wisdom today.
One is that of the ancient Greeks; the other is the Judeo-Christian
tradition. Our representative Greek thinker is Aristotle, who deployed
the concept in two distinct ways. On the one hand, Aristotle writes of
practical wisdom, or *phronēsis*, which describes deliberate action in
the world. Another wisdom, according to Aristotle, is *sophia*, which is
theoretical contemplation of things beyond our action.[5] (The Greek
sophia is where we get our word *philosophy*.) In essence, Aristotle presents a twofold understanding of wisdom that takes in both practical
reason and theoretical reason. This distinction between the different
kinds of wisdom is interesting in that it assumes that the nature of
wisdom alters depending on what it is directed toward. Driving a car?
Relating to your boss? Practical wisdom. Thinking about the divine?
Imagining eternity? Theoretical wisdom. Parts of the Bible are likely
influenced by this twofold Greek account of wisdom.[6] However,
what Aristotle and other Greek thinkers offer is not the same as the
picture the Bible gives us of wisdom.

In the Old and New Testaments, the Bible presents wisdom in
several different guises. In Job, wisdom is put forth as a solution to
the quandary that Job and his counselors have been working through
in the face of the immensity of Job's suffering. However, wisdom is
ultimately found to be as mysterious and elusive as any other solution.

---

4. Derek Kidner, *Proverbs*, Tyndale Old Testament Commentary (Downers Grove, IL:
IVP Academic, 2018), 22.

5. Aristotle, *Nicomachean Ethics*, 1139a3–8.

6. C. Wahlen, "Greek Wisdom," in *Dictionary of the Old Testament: Wisdom, Poetry &
Writings*, eds. Tremper Longman III and Peter Enns (Downers Grove, IL: IVP Academic,
2008), 842–43.

Getting wisdom is like mining for precious stones beneath the ground
(Job 28:1–12). Like miners of gold, seekers of wisdom must go to
incredible lengths to find wisdom. David F. Ford says of these verses
that "what the miners do is a profound and encouraging image for
those who are concerned with understanding the depths and dark-
nesses of the self, the world, and God."[7] Nevertheless, wisdom is
"hidden from the eyes of all living" (Job 28:21). Not even "Abaddon
and Death" have anything more to say than "we have heard a rumor
of it with our ears" (Job 28:22). The passage draws to a climax by
asserting that it is God who "understands the way to [wisdom], and
he knows its place" (Job 28:23). When he created all things, "he saw
it and declared it; he established it, and searched it out" (Job 28:27).
God is the source of wisdom and the one who knows where to find
it. To have wisdom, we must have access to God and his creation.

Proverbs is a basic guide to wisdom, whereas Job complicates the
picture painted by Proverbs. Job shows that even someone who "was
blameless and upright, one who feared God and turned away from
evil" is not immune to the world's unpredictable elements (Job 1:1).
While things might usually go in a particular way for most people
most of the time, Job, along with the book of Ecclesiastes, shows that
there are exceptions to the general rules of Proverbs and explores the
"limits of human life and knowledge."[8]

But the parallels are important as well. Like Job 28, Proverbs links
wisdom with creation. Proverbs 3, for example, uses similar imagery
to Job 28:

> The LORD by wisdom founded the earth;
>   by understanding he established the heavens;
> by his knowledge the deeps broke open,
>   and the clouds drop down the dew. (Prov 3:19–20)

---

7. David F. Ford, *Christian Wisdom: Desiring God and Learning in Love* (Cambridge:
Cambridge University Press, 2007), 137.

8. Raymond C. Van Leeuwen, "Wisdom Literature," in *Dictionary for Theological
Interpretation of the Bible*, ed. Kevin J. Vanhoozer, et al. (Grand Rapids: Baker Academic, 2005),
847.

So, too, Proverbs 8. Whereas in Proverbs 3 we see wisdom being instrumental in the creation of the world, Proverbs 8 presents wisdom as *created* and then participating in creation.

> Ages ago I was set up,
>> at the first, before the beginning of the earth.
> When there were no depths I was brought forth,
>> when there were no springs abounding with water.
> Before the mountains had been shaped,
>> before the hills, I was brought forth. (Prov 8:23–25)

Is this wisdom separate from God, or is it a part of God? Perhaps is it both? And what if this wisdom is also somehow Jesus Christ, for who else was present at the creation of all things?[9] I am not able to unpick all the difficult parts of these textual and theological debates, which go into matters well beyond the scope of this book. What I will assert is that this poetic passage maintains an important connection between both Jesus Christ and wisdom *and* creation and wisdom.[10] We will return to the question of Christ and wisdom soon, but for now, let us continue to explore the relationship between wisdom and creation.

Wisdom's depiction in Proverbs as being present at the creation is significant because it shows us that the structure of created reality is inherently linked to wisdom. Christians ought to hold that wisdom is linked to the way things are in actuality. Wisdom is at the bottom of the way the cosmos really is (Jer 10:12; Ps 104:24). This does not mean that we will always know how things actually are, of course. Our knowledge is limited and flawed in a variety of ways. But we can assert with confidence that all human action happens within the confines of a given order of things. As Raymond Van Leeuwen states, "Knowledge of the cosmic order requires knowledge … of how all things fit together and relate in one whole."[11] This links to my

---

9. Andrew Errington, *Every Good Path: Wisdom and Practical Reason in Christian Ethics and the Book of Proverbs* (London: T&T Clark, 2020), 99.

10. Quinn, *Walking in God's Wisdom*, 49.

11. Van Leeuwen, "Wisdom Literature," 849.

earlier framework for worldview education; the parts that we teach (or learn) fit into an ordered whole. Here we can see that the biblical conception of wisdom is inherently linked to this idea; wisdom is the ability to discern that order and how the parts fit together, even if our discernment is necessarily limited by our finiteness and sin.

Wisdom must also be put into action. It is never passive. Wisdom is never purely intellectual or rational. It is always ultimately ethical. The wise person acts in the world in accordance with the frame of the world. To be sure, wisdom is linked to knowledge in several biblical texts. A good example is Proverbs 2:1–3, 5–6:

> My son, if you receive my words
>   and treasure up my commandments with you,
> making your ear attentive to wisdom
>   and inclining your heart to understanding;
> yes, if you call out for insight
>   and raise your voice for understanding ...
> then you will understand the fear of the LORD
>   and find the knowledge of God.
> For the LORD gives wisdom;
>   from his mouth come knowledge and understanding.

A willing disposition toward "understanding" is a precondition for wisdom, and these are a precondition for possessing knowledge. The same point is made in Proverbs 2:10. If we submit ourselves to the wisdom that comes from God, then "wisdom will come into your heart, and knowledge will be pleasant for your soul."

Knowledge is also linked to action in Proverbs. It is never merely intellectual apprehension of, and organization of, data, something that more typical Christian worldview frameworks tend to emphasize. Instead, knowledge is something that is possessed and acted upon.[12] "Every prudent man acts with knowledge" (Prov 13:16). This practical emphasis is echoed in the New Testament in the book of James, which

---

12. Errington, *Every Good Path*, 108.

says that wisdom is shown in "good conduct" (Jas 3:13). The "wisdom from above is ... full of mercy and good fruits," resulting in a "harvest of righteousness" (Jas 3:17–18). Further, a pervasive image attached to wisdom in the Bible is that of house building.[13] "The wisest of women builds her house, but folly with her own hands tears it down" (Prov 14:1). Proverbs 24:3–4 says:

> By wisdom a house is built,
>   and by understanding it is established;
> by knowledge the rooms are filled
>   with all precious and pleasant riches.

Notice the use of wisdom, knowledge, and understanding in this passage, all in connection with that most practical of tasks: building a home. Constructing a house is an inherently practical matter, one that requires rational and practical wisdom. Indeed, the rational knowledge of house building is meaningless unless it is enacted. It is also more than simply the joining of timber. It is an act that constitutes a *household*, drawing people together under one roof, organizing them, and helping them be fruitful.[14] Just as "The LORD by wisdom founded the earth" (Prov 3:19), so people by wisdom build a house (cf. 1 Kgs 10:4–8; 2 Chr 9:3–7).[15]

The whole of reality is imbued with the wisdom of God and is structured by it. Therefore, all human action can be done in a way that is foolish or wise, whether the acts are acts of worship or other kinds of action. This is why Van Leeuwen talks about wisdom being

---

13. On this, I recommend Raymond C. Van Leeuwen, "Cosmos, Temple, House: Building and Wisdom in Ancient Mesopotamia and Israel," in *From the Foundations of Creation: Essays on Temple Building in the Ancient Near East and Hebrew Bible*, ed. Mark J. Boda and James Novotny (Tecklenburg, Germany: Ugarit-Verlag, 2010), 399–422. Also, Errington, *Every Good Path*, 100–102. The wider typological and symbolical parallels to house building and wood in the Bible are important also: see James B. Jordan, *Through New Eyes: Developing a Biblical View of the World* (Brentwood, TN: Wolgemuth & Hyatt, 1988), 81–94, and later chapters.

14. Errington, *Every Good Path*, 102.

15. Van Leeuwen, "Cosmos, Temple, House," 409–13, especially 413.

a "totality concept," for it is "as broad as reality and constitutes a culturally articulated way of relating to the entire world."[16]

But what is the relationship of this "totality concept" to creation? Proverbs 8 indicates that there is a close relationship between wisdom and the created order:

> The LORD possessed me at the beginning of his work. ...
> Ages ago I was set up,
>   at the first, before the beginning of the earth. ...
> When he marked out the foundations of the earth,
>   then I was beside him, like a master workman.
>
>   (Prov 8:22, 23, 29–30)

Wisdom appears to be something that is embedded in creation and, according to Gerhard Von Rad, "immanent in the world."[17]

But if wisdom is *in* the world, then how do we understand the connection between the wisdom of the world and the (potential) wisdom of human actions? Here I want to call on a fellow Australian scholar, Andrew Errington. In his study of the concepts of wisdom and practical reason in the book of Proverbs, Errington concludes that wisdom is "a kind of practical knowledge that arises out of the character of the world."[18] The world is made with wisdom as a part of its structure, meaning that human action needs to be concurrent with the structure of reality in order to be wise. Wisdom is, as Errington argues, "*other to us*," meaning that we still have to *get at it* somehow.[19] This is why Proverbs implores us to "get wisdom" (Prov 4:5, 7; 16:16). Wisdom is not inherent in people, but it is inherent in the creation. And that creation is, says Errington, "hospitable to good action."[20] The world

---

16. Van Leeuwen, "Wisdom Literature," 848.

17. Gerhard Von Rad, *Wisdom in Israel* (Harrisburg, PA: Trinity Press International, 1993), 145–54. Cf. the critique of this immanentist view of wisdom in Andrew Errington, *Every Good Path*, 95–97.

18. Errington, *Every Good Path*, 89.

19. Errington, *Every Good Path*, 103.

20. Errington, *Every Good Path*, 118.

is made in such a way that right action fits into it like a hand in a glove. The wisdom of the world receives the wise acts of a person and reveals the positive, constructive relationship "between the subject and the reality of the world."[21] The outcomes of wisdom result from this partnership between the order of reality and the wise person.

To summarize the Bible's presentation of wisdom, Quinn lists several helpful ingredients: it is an attribute of God and Christ, it is grounded in fearing God, it seeks to live in line with created reality, it lives out God's ways in particular contexts, and it is rooted in tradition.[22] As for a short definition, Brad Littlejohn calls it "the soul's attunement to reality."[23] This fits nicely with Bavinck's statement that "true wisdom ... has not to do with tenuous theories but with knowledge of reality."[24] When we are talking about wisdom from a Christian perspective, we are talking about something that is grounded in created reality, in an existing and given order.

Taking into account the other aspects of wisdom I have discussed in this section, my definition of wisdom is: seeing God's world properly, reading his word truly, and acting rightly in light of this. This definition takes into account the importance of apprehending God's created reality. If we don't understand the order of reality, then how do we know how to act? It also acknowledges the importance of properly reading God's special revelation for wisdom. Finally, the definition contains within it the necessity of connecting knowledge of reality and revelation with action. As I explain below, people don't need access to special revelation to act wisely in a general sense. All people have within them the capacity to become wise through their partial apprehension of created reality. But there is a sense in which knowing God and his word plays an important role in the formation of a wise person. The last section of the chapter will explore how

---

21. Errington, *Every Good Path* , 122.

22. Quinn, *Walking in God's Wisdom*, 9–16. Cf. Van Leeuwen, "Wisdom Literature," 848–49.

23. Bradford Littlejohn, *What's Wrong With "Worldview"?* (Moscow, ID: Davenant, 2018), 13.

24. *CW*, 50.

this definition of wisdom ought to be a central plank in a theory of Christian worldview education. But before we get to that, we must draw out one aspect of wisdom that we have yet to deal with at any length. And that is wisdom's connection to God.

Wisdom Refined

The connection between wisdom and God is a strong one in the Bible. The "fear" of God is repeatedly stated to be the foundation of wisdom (Job 28:28; Prov 9:10; Ps 111:10). So there is a sense in which the fullness of wisdom is available only to those who follow the words and ways of God. In Proverbs 2, in one of a series of father-to-son monologues in the opening chapters, the father says that "if you receive my words ... then you will understand the fear of the LORD and find the knowledge of God" (Prov 2:1, 5). Elizabeth H. P. Blackfish says that "seeking wisdom begins with fearing the Lord, which leads to knowing the Lord, which in turn results in receiving wisdom from its source."[25] The passage goes on to say that God "stores up sound wisdom for the upright" and "is a shield to those who walk in integrity" (Prov 2:7). And once someone fears God, it is then that they "will understand righteousness and justice and equity, every good path; for wisdom will come into your heart" (Prov 2:9–10). Does this mean that Christians will always be healthier, wealthier, and wiser than other people? Not at all. There is no compelling evidence of that in the world, nor does the Bible promise such a thing. Nevertheless, we must acknowledge that the Scriptures point to a special connection between faith and God blessing those who have faith with wisdom. Wisdom is a creation category, and we should affirm that wisdom is embedded in the order of reality and accessible to all people. But there is special access to wisdom for those who fear God.

Wisdom is also personified in the book of Proverbs in such a way that many Christian theologians have identified it with Jesus Christ.

---

25. Elizabeth H. P. Blackfish, "Biblical Wisdom as a Model for Christian Liberal Arts Education," *Christian Higher Education* 18, no. 5 (2019): 384.

Given the active role that the personified Wisdom in Proverbs 8 takes in the creation of the world and the correlations to texts like John 1:3 and Colossians 1:16, this conclusion is understandable. While I cannot resolve the questions about Proverbs 8 and Jesus Christ here, I can explore more generally how Christ is connected to wisdom in the Bible. And while I have dealt above with wisdom as a creation concept, in this section I will briefly address wisdom's connection with redemption. This discussion will begin to address a major quandary that Christian educators face when thinking about wisdom and worldview: How do we relate Christian education to those who might not have faith? Is Christian education for unbelievers also? I will return to this more fully in the following chapter, but this section will focus on showing how Jesus Christ manifests and embodies the creational wisdom described in the Old Testament.

In Ephesians 3, the apostle Paul explains his calling as an apostle and preacher to the Gentiles in order to provide his readers with confidence that the gospel they have received is genuine. Paul describes his mission "to preach to the Gentiles the unsearchable riches of Christ, and to bring to light for everyone what is the plan of the mystery hidden for ages in God" (Eph 3:8–9). Paul's mission is to reveal the "mystery" of the gospel, not in the sense that it cannot be understood, but as something that was previously hidden but is now unveiled. He does this "so that through the church the manifold wisdom of God might now be made known to the rulers and authorities in the heavenly places" (Eph 3:10). The preaching of this mystery gospel (now revealed) results in the revelation of God's wisdom to spiritual "rulers and authorities." Paul clarifies what this wisdom is in the next verse. According to Paul, God's actions in history, which are "according to his eternal purpose," are "realized in Christ Jesus our Lord" (Eph 3:11). The "manifold wisdom of God" is made known to the rulers and authorities (and presumably everyone else) through the life, death, resurrection, and ascension of Jesus Christ.

The connection between Christ and wisdom is made even more explicit in 1 Corinthians. In 1 Corinthians 1:24, Paul calls Jesus Christ "the wisdom of God." Why? As with Ephesians 3, he gives several revelatory reasons in this passage. He juxtaposes the Christian gospel of "the cross" with the "wisdom of the world" (1 Cor 1:18–20). The world is pursuing folly, and "in the wisdom of God, the world did not know God through wisdom" (1 Cor 1:21). Worldly wisdom looks the wrong way for salvation and spiritual wisdom, whereas "those who are called" know that "Christ is the power of God and the wisdom of God" (1 Cor 1:24). Indeed, those who are called are "in Christ Jesus," who by virtue of this union "became to us wisdom from God" (1 Cor 1:30).

It is clear from these passages that Jesus Christ is wisdom, and this wisdom is related to redemption rather than creation. Jesus Christ "became to us wisdom from God, righteousness and sanctification and redemption" (1 Cor 1:30). The redemptive purposes of God are realized in the person and work of Christ. This work of redemption was done in the created order, but the same work is fulfilled in the heavenly order (Heb 9:12). Christ died the death of a human being on a cross and yet completes this work by entering "not into holy places made with hands, which are copies of the true things, but into heaven itself, now to appear in the presence of God on our behalf" (Heb 9:24). Does this redemptive wisdom transcend and replace the wisdom of Job, Proverbs, and Ecclesiastes?

To answer this question, we must thread the needle through the biblical concept of wisdom. Notice that I didn't say *concepts*. There is only one wisdom: God's wisdom. That same wisdom manifested itself in creation as it did in redemption. Just as the Son of God was there at the creation of the world and continues to uphold all things (Col 1:16–17), so too Christ is the eternal Son who condescends to tabernacle with us and save us (John 1). God's works of creation and redemption unite in the person of Jesus Christ.[26] The wisdom of God built into the structure of reality is the same wisdom that broke into that structure to act decisively to redeem his people. There is a happy, if sometimes paradoxical, unity between the wisdom of creation and

---

26. Errington, *Every Good Path*, 200.

redemption, undergirded by the wisdom of "God's action in creation" apprehended by believers "in the light of Christ."[27] This does not disqualify non-Christians from discerning the order of wisdom in creation; it just means that the faithful see reality and act in it in light of redemption. The same wisdom, ultimately personified in Jesus Christ, permeates both creation and redemption.

Two Kinds of Wisdom

This conclusion that there is one wisdom does not nullify the possibility of there being two *types* of wisdom for those of us living and acting in creation. I want to close off this exploration of the definition of wisdom by briefly exploring these two types of wisdom from a biblical perspective.

The Bible offers us two forms of wisdom, both of which are accessible to humans. Both forms are important, and both are relevant in the context of Christian education. These two kinds are practical wisdom and spiritual wisdom. In a fundamental and theological sense, these two wisdoms are joined in the person of Jesus Christ. However, in another sense, they are separate in our experience of life under the sun. We all know people who exhibit practical wisdom and yet reject spiritual wisdom. Likewise, some are spiritually wise and yet lack practical wisdom. There is a distinction here, and it is important when framing the task of Christian education.

Practical wisdom is the wisdom evident in the person who knows a lot about living in the cosmos that God has created. It is exhibited in social and familial relationships, political activities, physical labor, scientific inquiry, learning and knowledge, and so on. This is the wisdom that we might even call "natural." It is grounded in the creation order, flows into a life that exhibits prudence in actions and words, and displays fruitfulness as an outworking. The practically wise person has a strong relationship with the creation.

---

27. Errington, *Every Good Path*, 201.

Spiritual wisdom, on the other hand, is connected to having a relationship with the Creator. The spiritually wise person knows God, loves his ways, loves his word, and pursues a life that is pleasing to him. She does this not just so she can flourish, but so that she can please him and glorify him. Spiritual wisdom also works itself out in a life that is bent toward serving others in the context of the people of God, the church. Spiritual wisdom bears spiritual fruit. A person can have both kinds of wisdom, and ideally we will all exhibit both practical and spiritual wisdom. They are not mutually exclusive, but you do not need one to have the other.

The Bible is full of descriptions of, and praise for, practical wisdom. This is the kind of wisdom that is discussed in Proverbs:

"He who gathers in summer is a prudent son." (Prov 10:5)

"The soul of the diligent is richly supplied." (Prov 13:4)

"The wisest of women builds her house." (Prov 14:1)

"The wisdom of the prudent is to discern his way." (Prov 14:8)

"Wisdom rests in the heart of a man of understanding." (Prov 14:33)

Practical wisdom is also evident in certain characters in the Bible. Joshua is said to have been "full of the spirit of wisdom, for Moses had laid his hands on him. So the people of Israel obeyed him and did as the LORD had commanded Moses" (Deut 34:9). Moses had commissioned Joshua to be his successor as ruler over the people of Israel. Earlier in Deuteronomy, Moses commanded the Israelites to select leaders in each tribe who were "wise, understanding, and experienced" (Deut 1:13). In Genesis, Joseph recommends to Pharoah that he select "a discerning and wise man" to oversee the distribution of goods during the preparation for the famine, as well as during the famine (Gen 41:33). Pharoah recognizes these qualities in Joseph and appoints him to this post (Gen 41:37–40).

Practical wisdom is also evident in the life of Solomon. Here, we see wise judgment and deliberation; "the wisdom of God was in him to do justice" (1 Kgs 3:28). Solomon had "wisdom and understanding beyond measure, and breadth of mind like the sand on the seashore" (1 Kgs 4:29). This "breadth of mind" manifested itself in lyrical and musical skill (1 Kgs 4:32), knowledge of zoology and botany (1 Kgs 4:33), and knowledge of building and architecture (1 Kgs 6). Indeed, Solomon is a model of practical wisdom (that is, until he forfeits this wisdom later in his life). He demonstrates to us the breadth of practical wisdom. It is a wisdom that stretches from a theoretical understanding of animals, justice, and architecture to a rich practical understanding of government administration. "Wisdom gives strength to the wise man more than ten rulers who are in a city" (Eccl 7:19).

While political rule is boosted by wisdom, so too is household management (Prov 31). Wisdom shows itself in good works and right conduct (Jas 3:13; Eph 5:15; Col 4:5). It also manifests itself in craftsmanship. Exodus 31 tells of two men, Bezalel and Oholiab, who are gifted by the Spirit of God to build and craft the tabernacle and the elements inside the tabernacle (Exod 31:1–8). God, by his Spirit, gave them "ability and intelligence, with knowledge and all craftsmanship" (Exod 31:3). Indeed, it says further that God gave "to all able men ability, that they may make all that I have commanded you" (Exod 31:6). Wisdom is of great practical benefit. As argued above, creation is hospitable to wise acts, and this works itself out in all the various spheres of human activity.

What of spiritual wisdom, then? As discussed above, Jesus Christ is "the wisdom of God" (1 Cor. 1:24), and God is immeasurably wise (Rom 11:33; Job 12:13; Rom 16:27, Isa 31:2). Humans can become spiritually wise because God's wisdom is handed down to humans in his word. Psalm 19:7 says that the law of the Lord "is perfect ... making wise the simple." Those who listen to what God says are wise (Pss 2:10; 94:8). The prophet Daniel says that those who have wisdom receive it from God (Dan 2:21). This is in contrast to the fool, who "says in his heart 'There is no God' " (Ps 14:1). Jesus uses the proverbial imagery of house building when he says the one who "hears these words of mine and does them will be like a wise man who built his house on the rock" (Matt 7:24). If hearing and doing the words of Jesus is a sign of wisdom (cf. Jas 1:22–25), then there is a wisdom that is particularly connected to spiritual matters.

This is further evident in the deployment of the wisdom concept throughout the New Testament. In the parable of the ten virgins, it is those who bring enough oil and are therefore properly prepared to wait for the returning bridegroom who are considered wise (Matt 25:4). The bridegroom in this parable is Jesus, meaning that the virgins' wisdom is not simply practical but is linked to a kind of spiritual discernment. In contrast, Paul describes those who "exchanged the glory of the immortal God for images resembling mortal man" and animals, those who reject God, as fools (Rom 1:22–23). They are the fools of Psalm 14:1. As we have seen, listening to and responding to the word of God is an entirely different matter. As Paul writes to Timothy, the Scriptures "are able to make you wise for salvation through faith in Christ Jesus" (2 Tim 3:15). There is a wisdom offered in God's word that is not practical, but spiritual. It is a wisdom that is garnered by hearing the words of God and by responding to these words with obedience and faith. We can be made "wise for salvation," and this work is done by the Holy Spirit working through the Scriptures and the message of the gospel.

Wisdom and Education

So far we have seen that wisdom is seeing God's world properly, reading his word truly, and acting rightly in light of this. From this, we can appreciate the importance of apprehending God's created reality and acting in light of this apprehension. We have also explored the connections between Jesus Christ as the "wisdom of God" and the wisdom expounded in books like Proverbs. This was all tied together by differentiating two kinds of biblical wisdom: practical wisdom and spiritual wisdom.

My claim in this last section of the chapter is that these two kinds of wisdom ought to be the substantial content of a Christian education. I want to explore how we might theoretically and practically link the pursuit of wisdom as it is laid out in the Scriptures with a Christian vision of education.

The entire book of Proverbs is framed as advice from parent to child. The parent offers the child teaching on how to live well in the world.

Hear, my son, your father's instruction,
and forsake not your mother's teaching. (Prov 1:8)

Whether one is a parent, a pastor, or in a teaching role in an educational institution, these verses apply. The child is a student sitting under the teaching of someone in authority who is preparing them to move into maturity.[28] The didactic task is framed in Proverbs as helping the student "find favor and good success in the sight of God and man" (Prov 3:4). Attentive learners are told they will "walk on [their] way securely, and [their] foot will not stumble" (Prov 3:23). The whole point of this teaching exercise is to provide the student with a foundation for righteousness and wisdom in a world that will (generally) accept it, and by which they will (generally) thrive in that world.

The setting of the book of Proverbs is informative also. Proverbs is situated in a covenant community. It is composed in the context of a community of faith and presumes a common set of metaphysical convictions, while simultaneously offering pieces of advice that aren't inherently connected to those convictions. Everyone knows that unjust weights are, well, unjust, despite the variety of religious convictions in the world. So there is a confessional particularity to the setting and generality to the content.

Wisdom teaching is not confined to Proverbs, of course, but these two observations help us frame Christian education in light of the Bible's understanding of wisdom. First, education ought to be understood as the presentation of, imparting of, and pursuit of wisdom.

---

28. Mark Hinds, "Teaching for Responsibility: Confirmation and the Book of Proverbs," *Religious Education* 93, no. 2 (1998): 211.

What could be more satisfying to a teacher than seeing a student emerge equipped with wisdom? Much of the "content" of education can be classified under practical wisdom. When we are teaching students about mathematics, we are helping them gain wisdom about the mathematical order of reality. When we teach students physical education, they are gaining theoretical wisdom about the way their bodies work and practical wisdom about how to use their bodies. When we teach students about history, they gain wisdom about the ways of humankind, human civilizations, and a sense of the scale and complexity of human existence. This gives them wisdom about their own world and about why the world is the way it is. It also offers them perspective on what they cannot know, given that much is hidden in history, which is also formative of wisdom.

In an education seen through the lens of practical wisdom, students are gaining an understanding of the world and of reality through the gaining of knowledge and skills that will help them live a wise and fruitful life in the creation of God. Creation is, in Errington's words, "hospitable to the successful living of human life."[29] An education that is shaped by the teaching and pursuing of wisdom leads students toward this kind of success. It is not necessarily the success that the world loves to see, such as a healthy bank account and career seniority, but is rather a life marked by a right understanding of reality.

Truth about reality, about the world that God has made, is not confessionally determined. We are not limited in our epistemology by our religious commitments. Therefore, the scope of education can be as wide and deep as God's world is.

At the same time, Christian education will inevitably revolve around a particular religious confession. This means there will be a Christian element to a Christian education. A vision for education shaped by the Christian understanding of wisdom naturally incorporates the spiritual elements of wisdom. There is, after all, a knowledge that "makes you wise for salvation," which Paul talks about in

---

29. Errington, *Every Good Path*, 131.

his letter to Timothy (2 Tim 3:15). A Christian education that has wisdom at its core ought to incorporate the inculcation of the faith as part of its program.

Spiritual wisdom is of a different kind than practical wisdom, and while they are connected, they cannot be gained in the same way. The integration of faith with practical wisdom is much more a task for the learner than the teacher. Whether the students will pursue the spiritual wisdom held out to them in Jesus Christ isn't something we can control. But we can and should be purveyors of that wisdom if we are Christian educators. These bits of wisdom are like the tiles on a big, glorious mosaic. As mosaic laborers, students and teachers do not have access to the master plan. They do not know the final picture. But they can proceed with confidence, knowing that they are pursuing the truth about the little tiles of reality that they are called to work on.

Conclusion

This vision for an education shaped around the biblical understanding of wisdom provides us with a fuller picture of the metaphor of the worldview mosaic. Teachers and students cannot see the entire mosaic of a Christian worldview; the finished piece of art is in the mind of God alone. However, we can imagine ourselves as workers on the mosaic of created reality. We don't create reality, but when we come to access the wisdom that is embedded in the warp and woof of creation, it is as though we grasp one tile and place it correctly.

There is an important distinction between my approach to these questions of worldview and other worldview education theorists that is helpfully illustrated by Andrew Errington. He points out that wisdom "resides in the distinct, concrete realities of God's work of creation and reconciliation, and not in an overarching account of how they fit together."[30] Wisdom is found in knowledge of God's world and in knowing God as Savior. The focus of wisdom is not on the discernment of an overarching system, which is how Christians

---

30. Errington, *Every Good Path*, 133.

have usually understood worldview. The same could be said for the understanding of Christian education that I am arguing for. While we are talking in terms of worldview, our grasp of that worldview is necessarily limited, and therefore the normative force of the world-view idea is blunted. Rather than pursuing an overarching account of how everything fits together, Christian students and teachers ought to pursue the wisdom of God and of his creation in the little pieces of reality that are right in front of them. My argument in the next chapter is that doing so will constitute a wider and richer education in the truths of God's world and God's word.

Chapter 5

When Do We Arrive?
Reaching for Reality

What would it be like to come to a strange city, say London, with only a map of the underground subway system? You may know you need to get from Watford to Crystal Palace, and all you have on your map is a bewildering network of subway stations. The map tells you something about your route, though. It appears you need to head southeast, and it is likely not a short journey. But how can you tell for sure? What obstacles lie in your way if you journey on foot? Is there a tram that will take you there? And is the way undulating? Are there any bodies of water between you and your destination? Perhaps there are mountains, or a dangerous forest. The underground map gives you some information about your route, but very little. What you need is to see a fuller picture. You need a comprehensive map that includes topography, information about hills and rivers and so on, and topology, such as that on the subway map. But that will only help you to an extent. To really know where to go and how to get there, you need knowledge of the city along with the practical know-how of how to get around. You need a comprehensive map along with practical experience to get you to Crystal Palace in the best way possible.

The work of educating for a Christian worldview is like the work of mapmaking.[1] In the mapmaking process, you are looking to create the best map you can to help people get to where they need to go. The completed map is like a Christian worldview that contains all the elements of life's topology and topography, an accumulation of wisdom for the task of living in God's world. The aim of Christian education is to apprehend reality in all its elements: God, self, and the world. In reaching for this reality through the gradual gathering of wisdom, Christian educators are giving students the gift of a Christian worldview. This chapter aims to explain how these different aspects work together to complete the Christian education project.

I am not the first person to bring worldview and wisdom together. J. Mark Bertrand, in his book (Re)thinking Worldview, suggests that worldview is the foundation of wisdom.[2] Bertrand was on the right track in partnering these concepts, but I think he got them the wrong way around; wisdom is the foundation of worldview. Benjamin Quinn has also brought wisdom and worldview together in his study on the book of Proverbs, claiming that wisdom is "the clue to worldview" and arguing that wisdom is "the proper lens through which" we can "discern how to properly live in the Creator's world."[3] Quinn is closer to the mark than Bertrand, but I want to refine the connection between wisdom and worldview even further. A person who has imbibed, internalized, and acts on Christian wisdom, wisdom that rests upon truth about self, God, and the world, has a Christian worldview. Any understanding of Christian worldview ought to rest upon wisdom. Wisdom is not a lens; wisdom is the tiles that make up the worldview mosaic. Wisdom is the lines on the worldview map that show us how to live.

1. See James Eglinton, "Editor's Introduction," in PW, 13.

2. J. Mark Bertrand, (Re)thinking Worldview: Learning to Think, Live and Speak in This World (Wheaton, IL: Crossway, 2007), 109–20.

3. Quinn, Walking in God's Wisdom, 17–26.

Furthermore, I want to drag us away from the sort of deductive Christian worldview thinking that suggests we can attain a singular, uninhibited vision of reality. Such a vision rests only with God, and even then, there are as many worldviews as there are people. The idea that there is one "lens" or one overarching "view" of things that we are imparting in Christian educational contexts is deeply problematic. Therefore, the normative power we attach to this conception of worldview becomes arbitrary and hubristic. Instead of asking whether such-and-such fits within the confines of a Christian worldview education, we ought to ask different questions and use different frameworks.

This chapter seeks to draw together each of the aspects from the former chapters to paint a different vision of Christian worldview education from the ones that currently exist. Happily, this vision does not constitute a revolution in the content of Christianity or of what we might consider Christian. Nevertheless, certain emphases and approaches readily flow out from my reimagining of worldview. I want to challenge the philosophical and theological foundations of Christian worldview education. In doing so, I hope to provide practitioners, pastors, teachers, lecturers, students, and parents with a richer vision of what a Christian worldview education means for both disciples and teachers. Rather than seeing worldview education as trying to fit content within the constraints of a preconceived intellectual system, we ought to see it as the pursuit of the real. In Christian education, we ought to see ourselves as reaching for reality and helping others to do the same.

Christian Education as Mosaic Building

Worldview metaphors, and the term "worldview" itself, usually imply that the problem is one of vision. If we can just see everything properly, we will be fine. Education becomes the process of clearing the fog, cleaning the window, or selecting the correct glasses; we can fix our worldview by fixing our perspective. There is some truth to this idea, but it is deceptively simple to suggest (a) that we might grasp reality, or view the "world," comprehensively and (b) that the problem is one of our "view" of things. These two implications of the optical imagery of worldview should be set aside. As I argued in chapter 3, we should instead think about worldview formation as a constructive process that is imperfect and incomplete, but nevertheless is reaching for something true. As Christians, we believe in a coherent reality that is accessible and orderly.

This orderly, accessible reality is the mosaic. It is the "world" in worldview. As learners and teachers, we have only an imperfect grasp of the larger mosaic. The mosaicist of the Mausoleum of Galla Placidia would have had a team of people helping him prepare the surfaces and cut and lay the *tesserae*. But this team of people would not necessarily have had much of an idea about the big picture of the mosaic. It was the mosaicist who held this pivotal information in his mind and on the master plan. So, while we might have some sense of the overall plan of the Christian worldview, as learners and teachers our view is limited. It is only God who possesses the entire, perfect view of reality. It is our job to try and ascertain the truth about that reality in whatever limited manner we can.

In chapter 3, I argued that we should shift away from the common understanding of worldview and embrace one that is rooted in Christian critical realism. This entailed a conviction that the overall mosaic is orderly, meaningful, and something we can find out about. I also argued that the process of learning about the mosaic is inductive; that is, we learn piece by piece. We don't start with a detailed account of reality and ascertain what we are supposed to make of all the details within this larger framework. The larger framework is skeletal in our own understanding, at best. We might see some of the master mosaicist's etchings on the ceiling and the walls, and we might know that something beautiful is taking shape. We know there is a plan, and we can discern some limited aspects of that overall plan. But we don't know much. And so our task as learners and educators is to build on the picture, to put together the different aspects of the mosaic, piece by piece, tile by tile. If your job is to teach chemistry, then teach chemistry as well as you can, with the best tools you can, to the glory of God. That is your job because your task fits into a bigger project.

Teachers and learners are part of a team of mosaic artists piecing together a Christian worldview. This is a wonderful thing because it means that educators don't need to have mastered the whole mosaic. No one on earth has the job of the master artist. Educators are to grasp their own corner of reality as well as they can and then help others do the same. Students and learners obviously won't have anywhere near a complete Christian worldview, and it is the same for educators. Teachers might have one corner or a couple of segments of the mosaic under their metaphorical control. But at the end of the day, educators are not master artisans. No one, not even the brightest astrophysicist or the most brilliant philosopher, has the mosaic within his grasp. Rather, educators are working on their own segment and passing on their knowledge of that to others. The chemistry teacher can focus on fruitfulness in her own corner of the school curriculum, helping her students understand and love the chemical structures of God's world through imparting the most credible scientific information she can. In doing this, she is helping students piece together their worldview through passing on wisdom, helping them discover the wisdom of the world. She doesn't need to have a devotional element to her class, and she doesn't need to spiritualize chemistry. Chemistry is already spiritual because the world is made by a Creator who designs and sustains all things. You don't need to insert the worldview key into your chemistry curriculum to make it more Christian, because God is already there! And by teaching his truth you are already building the worldviews of your students.

In Chapter 4, I proposed a new approach to thinking about the content of a worldview. Rather than seeing a worldview as a series of propositional statements, a formal philosophical framework, or even a mix of narratives and convictions, I suggested that a worldview is built by growing in wisdom. This understanding of worldview reflects, in my view, the nature of God's creation and our interaction with it.

Rather than seeing ourselves as standing back from the world and "viewing" it, we must understand that we are embodied creatures who dwell and act in God's world. Our thought and activity in the created order are reflective of a more or less accurate grasp of reality. Wise people are those who have learned the ways of God, and the warp and woof of God's world. They have also learned about themselves and how they relate to the world and God. They have become wise in the biblical sense because they can act in a way that the creation will be hospitable toward. They don't necessarily have their worldview system worked out. Nor do they have all the answers to respond to modernist, pantheist, or new age claims about the world. What the wise person has is a well-ordered understanding of reality that shapes her actions, a view shaped by the wisdom that is held out to her in creation and the Scriptures.

Educators, be they pastors, parents, teachers, or lecturers, have the vital job of partnering with learners in the quest for wisdom. Christian educators join with students in building their Christian worldview mosaic by giving them tiles to place. Each *tessera* is a piece of wisdom that helps build the mosaic. Each piece of wisdom that is passed on to students helps them construct their Christian worldview. For mathematics teachers, the question isn't "How do I teach this from a Christian perspective?" Rather, they ought to be asking "How do I make my students wise in mathematics?" Ancient history teachers should be asking "How do I help my students gain wisdom about the world and the human condition? And how can they learn from the historical examples I am presenting?" Simply teaching the facts of ancient history is a noble task, too, for history is the site and source of much wisdom. Rather than forcing Christianity into the content, educators ought to ask how their teaching will help students think and act wisely in God's world. How can this teaching enlighten the students' understanding of the relationship between themselves and others? To recall Charlotte Mason's language: What is it about this class that will help them take hold of the relations that exist in the world? Asking this kind of question can help educators align their content and their pedagogy with the aim of imparting wisdom, a wisdom that will build toward a Christian worldview.

Worldview is the goal of Christian education. For too long worldview has been seen as the means; it has been purported to be the *way* that students get a Christian education. Christian schools and colleges, along with apologetics and student ministries, all commonly claim to be teaching from a "Christian worldview" perspective. This implies there is a right way of viewing the world: the Christian way. The problem, according to many Christian thinkers, is that too often people are led astray into incorrect ways of thinking. They are led astray by the culture, media, and their non-believing friends or family, resulting in them having an un-Christian worldview. The proposed solution is to train people to think through everything from a Christian worldview perspective. In other words, the solution is to offer correctives to the false worldviews that are dominant around us. And one key way of doing that is to provide a Christian worldview education, an education that is filled with Christian worldview content. That is, in a nutshell, the old deductive way of thinking about Christian worldview education.

I have been arguing that this is unhelpful and unworkable. The deductive approach to Christian worldview needs to be set aside, and instead we ought to embrace the inductive approach. Worldview is the goal. The Christian worldview ought to be the *telos* of Christian education. We want students to leave our institutions with worldviews that are more Christian than when they arrived. And to do that, we need to offer them wisdom instead of worldview. Worldview doesn't work as a means, but it is a wonderful goal. Educators build the mosaic alongside the students, giving them wisdom tiles to place, and working with them toward the glorious vision of life that constitutes a Christian worldview. This is our core task as Christian educators. We are to partner with students in the construction of the mosaic of the Christian understanding of reality.

Of Mosaics and Curricula

Thus far, I have been making the case for a rethinking of worldview that emphasizes the inductive nature of education, the limitations of human knowledge, and a reconsideration of how worldview functions as a normative tool. Several questions and objections might arise from the argument: Am I saying that there are no deductive categories and truths that educators use in their teaching? Do we need to abandon the idea that teachers have a better-formed Christian worldview than their students? And if there is no complete Christian worldview attainable for mere humans, do Christian schools and colleges need to put aside Christian distinctives? It may seem from the foregoing argument that I am embracing a skeptical approach to knowledge that leads to a formless and even content-less Christian education. This Christian education appears to be a blob that is all flesh and no bones.

While I will not pretend to answer all comers, I want to broadly address these types of concerns and provide some balance to the argument of the book. First and foremost, the last thing Christian education institutions should do is abandon distinctives, especially those grounded in the Scriptures. The Bible is perspicuous; it contains clear teaching that can and should be applied across a range of issues that affect the form and content of Christian education. I heartily affirm the Westminster Confession's statement that the Scriptures contain the "whole counsel of God, concerning all things necessary for his own glory, man's salvation, faith and life."[4] Furthermore, these truths are "either expressly set down in Scripture," or humans can draw them out of the Scriptures "by good and necessary consequence."[5] The apostle Paul says in 2 Timothy 3:15–17 that the Bible has everything we need to "make [us] wise for salvation," that the Scriptures are foundational for "teaching," for "reproof," for "correction," and that they are useful for training people to be righteous and "equipped for

---

4. *Westminster Confession of Faith* (1647), chapter I, paragraph VI.

5. *Westminster Confession*, I.VI.

every good work." There is no way of looking at these verses and concluding that the Bible is not useful for education.

That means that the doctrinal truths about a whole range of issues will necessarily form a part of a Christian school's framework for their distinctives, and Christian teachers will necessarily deploy these truths in the classroom. Granting some flexibility on certain issues is important, as not every Christian agrees on every detail. But some issues, including hot-button ones like the binary nature of biological sex and gender, do have clear grounding in biblical teaching. Some institutions might want to adopt a young-Earth creationist view with regard to history and science, while others might allow some variation on this. A more black-and-white issue is the historicity of Jesus of Nazareth and his bodily resurrection. So, too, is the doctrine of the image of God, which grounds a number of topics covered in schools and colleges in a Christian understanding of humankind. This is all to say that the Bible offers us clear teaching on a number of issues that could be considered a part of a Christian worldview. These truths should be affirmed and ought to form a part of a school's or college's identity and doctrinal framework.

This leads to a second objection to do with the inductive-deductive distinction. Is it possible to teach everything with an inductive approach? Also, is it desirable? The answer to both questions must be "No." Teaching and instruction always start with some deductive categories. Teachers and lecturers will often have advanced knowledge of the topic at hand that will provide them with scaffolding they can use as they impart their knowledge to the students. Further, to have no scaffolding, no deductive categories, within which to inductively build knowledge would be almost unworkable. Perhaps exclusively focusing on inductive discovery as a method could work for some topics. However, this generally won't be the case.

In short, some boundaries, distinctives, and deductive categories are inevitably going to play a role in framing Christian education institutions and Christian classrooms. My purpose is not to dismiss this reality, but rather to push us to rediscover the true nature of Christian education, which is a journey of worldview building by growing in wisdom. To recapture this in theory and in practice requires a realignment in our thinking; we need to shift our thinking away from dogmatic worldview thinking and toward a Christian education that focuses on wisdom and developing a worldview.

These qualifications aside, one important implication of my reframing of Christian worldview in relation to education is that it reduces the normative edge of the worldview concept. As we have seen, this normative edge, which shows up as guiding prescriptions on who teaches and what is taught, cannot be applied in the same way if we understand worldview as inductive rather than deductive. Because we're no longer starting with high-level worldview principles and then deducing the consequences of them for curriculum and content, we need to rethink how we apply worldview in institutional settings. Because we are now seeing the student's worldview as a constructive project that we cannot discern the final design of, we are freed up to rethink many of the assumptions about the "Christian-ness" of our curriculum and teaching content. What counts as Christian? Does it need to quote the Bible to be Christian? Does it need a special Christian worldview framework that shows us how it is Christian? These questions are not irrelevant. But they aren't as important if we consider education as the process of growth in wisdom rather than a worldview "download." Such a reframing also provides an opportunity to examine how to think about Christian content in our syllabi. Rather than finding a Christian worldview take on each subject, which can be a compromise on quality, find the richest Christian texts and ideas and use them where they fit best. This will help bolster your students' Christian worldviews in a far more effective way than using a subpar, but Christian, textbook. I will expand on this below.

Another important implication directly affects those on the ground in Christian education. Whatever your setting, you should be permitted to teach your discipline and to teach it well. The old-style worldview-thinking doesn't need to permeate your content, your syllabus, and your curriculum plan. Rather, what should be seen everywhere is excellence. Teach what you know in a way that honors God and honors your students. You have permission (from me, at least!) to stop trying to force Christianity into every class with Bible verses, theological frameworks, and apologetics. Look for opportunities to add substantial Christian influences into what you're doing, to be sure (more on this below). But relax! Your main job is to impart wisdom by teaching truth and teaching well, whatever form that comes in. You are helping students place wisdom tiles first and foremost. The Christian worldview is the goal, the *telos*, not the means.

Several prescriptions flow out from these observations about institutions and educators. First, let us consider content and curriculum. If worldview formation is, as I have argued, an inductive process driven by the gradual accumulation of knowledge, then the very idea that we would teach history, chemistry, or physical education from the perspective of a Christian worldview is redundant. The deductive vision of a Christian worldview, I have argued, is an incomplete, vastly inadequate, account stemming from certain Christian intellectuals about the supposed boundaries around a discipline. Those who claim to have a, or *the*, Christian worldview perspective on any subject or discipline are claiming to possess the deductive framework within which, or from which, all the learning about that discipline flows. But we have seen that this is a difficult thing to sustain, and in an educational context we ought to think in very different terms.

Note well that I am not arguing for a value-neutral or secular framework for education content (as if such a thing were possible!). Rather, I am suggesting that the same reasoning that would cause us to reject the assumption of religious or ideological neutrality when it comes to education would also cause us to reject prescriptive worldview reasoning. We simply don't have all the answers, so how can we determine what ought to be inside or outside the Christian worldview box, in terms of content? If we are unable to make this determination, can we find a method of shaping a truly Christian way of educating in terms of content? I believe we can. It is a method that requires epistemic humility and might even invite levels of discomfort in terms of

what we deem "Christian." But this is a good thing because we ought
to be in the business of teaching wisdom, not dictating to people what
belongs in the Christian worldview box and what doesn't.

Another thing I will refrain from doing is dictating a particular
theological framework for determining the "worldview status" of
teaching content.[6] While this approach can bear some good fruit by
helping educators think with biblical and theological categories about
the content in their syllabus, it also contains some pitfalls. One big one
is the temptation to try and fit everything into a preconceived theological paradigm such as Creation-Fall-Redemption-Consummation.[7]
This can lead to problems whereby the specific content of a given unit
of study or discipline is subject to the rather arbitrary constraints of
the given biblical-theological framework. While one can certainly
profitably read the Scriptures in this way, these frameworks are often
alien to the subjects of study in an educational setting. Trying to
conform, say, civics or biology to a theological narrative framework
like this can quickly undermine the intellectual integrity of the education process. Similarly, subjects like ancient Greek mythology and
history can be quickly ruined by forcing them through the sieve of
one of the many deductive Christian worldview frameworks. Rather
than making the content fit the worldview framework or theological paradigm, prepare the student to read wisely. Teach them to be
discerning and critical rather than giving them all the pre-prepared
worldview answers.[8]

I will come to my positive prescriptions for Christian worldview
teaching soon, but allow me to make one more important comment,

---

6. An example of this approach comes from Christian Education National in Australia:
Ken Dickens et al., *Transformation by Design: The Big Picture* (Springwood, NSW: National
Institute for Christian Education, 2017). This guidebook is admirable in many ways but still
falls into the traps I'm suggesting we need to avoid.

7. E.g., Christian Schools Australia's *God's Big Story* suite.

8. The issue is not dissimilar to that of the critical theory approach that we see in schools
and universities. Framing all subjects with race, gender, and sexuality does violence to the
learning process, and it seems Christian worldview advocates are sometimes making an anal-
ogous mistake.

this time on the use of the Scriptures in Christian education settings. The Bible is, without question, the very word of God. It is written for our profit so that we might be saved, sanctified, and made wise. However, this does not mean that the Bible speaks to everything that we may teach about in the classroom, in the pulpit, or in the lecture theater. I distinctly remember the day when someone pointed out to me that the Bible does not mention this thing called a "Nintendo 64." Of course, the Scriptures provide tools for us to grow in wisdom and godliness concerning using things like video games. But we don't have prooftexts that mention them. The same is true with much of the content that is delivered in an education context. Aside from the teaching of the Bible and doctrine, the Scriptures offer limited resources for the Christian teacher.

Because of this fact, we need to use the Bible with great care. It is not something we should force into spaces where it doesn't fit, nor should it provide fodder to make us feel that we're using Christian worldview thinking. We might feel we can tick the worldview box by using a verse that mentions the topic or theme of the class, just so we can ensure there is Christian content. But the problems with this should be obvious. Unless the verse really helps us reach the goals of building up our students in wisdom, does it belong there? The following extract from a website about a Christian curriculum for science education says it very well:

> We assume that Christian parents already make Bible study
> an integral and essential part of the child's daily schedule. We
> believe that science, for Christians, is simply observing and
> truthfully describing God's creation. Our books are carefully
> selected to provide marvelous examples of all of the wonders
> of His creation. Our curriculum is written to provide a frame-
> work for an organized study of science, not as a tool to provide
> our own commentary. If science is viewed from a Christian
> perspective, then His invisible qualities will be clearly seen
> (Romans 1:20) without any need for comments from us.

We have also chosen not to include Scriptural references
in our materials outside of the introductions. Many science
programs are being marketed as Christian homeschool science
because they have sprinkled in a Bible verse here and there.
Some of these programs use verses that are clearly taken out
of context. In our opinion, it is unacceptable to teach children
to mold Scripture to fit our needs rather than allowing it to
teach us in context. We instead recommend that a complete,
sound Bible study be used in conjunction with our curriculum (or any other).[9]

I quote this at length because the philosophy behind this statement
incorporates several of the aspects of learning discussed so far in this
book. It also treats Scripture and the learner with dignity. Students of
science don't need a Bible verse to help them see truth about God's
creation; they need to have a high-quality science education and
learn to see and interpret the world well. And while "sprinkling" the
Scriptures is well-intentioned, it dishonors God's word by using it
in ways for which it was never intended. You might feel that you're
guarding against slipping into a different worldview perspective by
using the Bible as much as possible. It might be part of your tactics to
push back against unbelieving worldviews. But reverence for God's
word should give us pause whenever we risk deploying it in ways
alien to its core purpose.

Enough criticism, though. What can we do instead? First, consider the sources for a Christian worldview education. These sources
are sources of *wisdom*. We are reimagining worldview education as a
mosaic-building project, where the student and teachers join together
in finding and placing tiles of wisdom on the mosaic. Those tiles are
aspects of truth and knowledge about God's world, God, and ourselves. Thinking about worldview education in this way offers us an
opportunity to draw on sources of wisdom in a new way. To help

---

9. Noeo Science, "FAQs," https://noeoscience.com/pages/faqs.

us think about this, I have broken the sources of wisdom down into three kinds: scriptural, Christian, and general.

Scriptural. The first source of wisdom is the Scriptures contained in the Old and New Testaments. Despite the hesitations articulated above, the Bible remains a core source of wisdom about ourselves, God, and God's world. The main way that the Bible should be deployed in Christian education settings is in classes about Christianity. That is, the Bible should be liberally used in classes that might be categorized as catechesis, Bible study, or Christian studies. There are parts of the Bible that speak to matters beyond Christian doctrine, of course. Taking into account the warnings above, Christian educators should still feel excited by the prospect of applying God's word to enrich their students' Christian worldview beyond the realms of doctrine and Bible study. Nevertheless, the main way that Scripture should be used is to teach the doctrines of the faith and to teach the story of the Bible.

Christian. The second source of wisdom is that of our fellow Christians. The church is blessed with a rich and deep font of wisdom from the pens and minds of our fellow believers. This spans many academic disciplines and contributors, including some of the greatest minds in history. Christians have thought hard about any number of topics, from natural sciences, to politics, to law, to literature, to philosophy, to history, and beyond. The irony is that some of these works might not pass the "Christian worldview" test. But this shouldn't scare us off at all. The great minds of the faith have always pursued wisdom and knowledge beyond the confines of theology, and we ought to be ready to take advantage of this thinking. Likewise, we ought to think about how our disciplines might lend themselves to the study of great Christian texts. Literature is a rich example. Christian institutions and families can prioritize the reading of classics of the Christian world, from Augustine's *Confessions* to Milton's *Paradise Lost*, from Dante's *Inferno* to Graham Greene's *The Power and the Glory*. These are mere examples, and thankfully we are tremendously blessed with rich and thoughtful contributions that dwell on Christian themes and offer distinctly Christian perspectives across a range of disciplines.

General. The final source of wisdom is the wisdom of the world. This might seem to cut against scriptural injunctions *against* worldly wisdom. I am not at all intending to call those warnings into question, nor do I want to encourage people to run off and pursue destructive educational practices! I merely want Christian educators to acknowledge that there is remarkable wisdom and great value in the non-Christian world. As I have said, Christians do not have a monopoly on academic knowledge or wisdom. Rather than thinking in terms of "Christian" and "non-Christian," we ought to consider the "closeness of relation" that the matter under consideration has to our relationship to God and our understanding of the human person.[10] The closer the relation, the more care and discernment are required in using unbelieving sources. For example, the discipline of psychology, which reaches into the heart of what it means to be a human person made in the image of God, requires a great deal of care. The Bible speaks quite clearly about the human person and the impact of sin and holiness on the human psyche and our experience of the world. Another pertinent example is biology and anatomy, which in the current day are areas of great controversy in relation to sex and gender. These issues are, in my view, much more important than debates about the age the of the earth or the origins of different biological species, because they touch on the human person and the image of God.

However, there is much in the world of knowledge and learning that lies far away from those matters. Other matters, such as physical education or mathematics, have almost no relation to distinctively Christian thinking and require less care in this regard. Disciplines such as law, literature, social sciences, and history are more ambiguous, and the approach you take will depend on the content or themes you are dealing with at the time. These subjects and disciplines open

---

10. Emil Brunner, *Revelation and Reason: The Christian Doctrine of Faith and Knowledge*, trans. Olive Wyon (London: SCM, 1947), 383.

up real opportunities for the discerning use of non-Christian sources. Those outside the church have achieved great things and discovered wonderful insights into the way humans are and the way the world is. John Calvin puts it well when he says that there is a "universal apprehension of reason and understanding by nature implanted" in all humankind, such that abilities in "the arts and sciences" are "bestowed indiscriminately upon pious and impious."[11] He goes even further when he asserts that "secular writers," despite the fall and sin, are blessed with the "admirable light of truth." Calvin says that "we cannot read the writings of the ancients on" subjects such as medicine, law, mathematics, philosophy, and biology "without great admiration."[12] Why? Because "the Spirit of God" is "the sole fountain of truth," and in acknowledging truth wherever we find it we honor God and the gifts he has given to humankind.[13] Non-Christians may not know the one true God, except in a limited way (Rom 1:19), but even so they can know quite a lot about his creation. According to Calvin, they can be "sharp and penetrating in their investigation of inferior things," that is, of things that have a more distant relation to the core truths of the faith.

Because we are pursuing wisdom, and all truth is indeed God's, we need not be afraid of what the world has to offer. We can prayerfully seek truth outside the church and rejoice at the ways that non-Christians who discover truth and advance wisdom can contribute to the formation of Christian worldviews.

Practical Outworkings

I want to draw all of this together by offering some practical prescriptions in light of this way of thinking about content and curriculum. Some of these suggestions affect policy, while some will affect the way

---

11. John Calvin, *Institutes of the Christian Religion*, ed. John T. McNeill, trans. Ford Lewis Battles (Louisville: Westminster John Knox, 2006), 2.2.14.

12. Calvin, *Institutes*, 2.2.15.

13. Calvin, *Institutes*, 2.2.15.

we teach. Certain things will practically flow out of the new framework articulated above, and I will expand on some here.

First, we should think about forming Christian thinkers through
catechesis. This could look different in different contexts, but I believe
one overriding principle should be adopted: Christian education institutions should formally teach their students doctrine and Bible. Under
the old worldview framework, Christianity is understood to be everywhere and in everything. This old way of thinking is not a problem
per se, but it has resulted in a dilution of the faith as it is presented
in Christian education. Even when there is a Christian core, the fact
that Christianity is apparently through all the institution's curriculum
means that the core can quickly become an ideological and apologetic
tool so that everything is filtered through a worldview lens. Such an
approach can result in an unsystematic presentation shaped more by
the demands of the surrounding secular culture than by the Scriptures
and traditions of Christianity. Rather than presenting Christianity
and the message of Christ, we too often put on an anti-world front.
We adopt the defensive stance I mentioned in the opening chapter. We often teach *against* what we perceive to be un-Christian. But
does doing so serve students well? Does it prepare them to think for
themselves and really address the poisonous and false ideas and ide-
ologies of the world?

A better approach is to present the positive message of Christianity
and deliberately ground students in the faith. That requires catechesis.
If we are serious about shaping thinkers in a truly Christian way,
the foundations for this must be basic doctrine and knowledge of
the Bible. Christian institutions, whether they have churched or
unchurched students, ought to be unapologetic about this emphasis
and provide classes that teach students the basic heads of Christian
doctrine, from the doctrine of God through to eschatology. They
also ought to have students study the Scriptures and learn the biblical story. This means that, rather than spreading "Christian studies"
across the teaching body of the school and across all subjects, students
ought to be taught doctrine and Bible by people who have formally

studied these subjects. Those who teach doctrine and Scripture ought to really know what they're doing so that students are grounded in the basic tenets of the faith. This grounding will become the basis for the gathering of wisdom, for the building of the mosaic, in the rest of the disciplines. Again, the implication is not that those who know Christian doctrine are better students of every other area of study, but rather that those who know the fundamentals of the faith will be better prepared to apply the faith in different intellectual and practical contexts. The current approach often results in students who are ready with the worldview-related answers, but ill-equipped with the basics of Christianity.

The second prescription that flows from what I have argued thus far is this: the cultivation of wisdom for a Christian worldview involves the formation of Christian imaginations through great books. The questions that are raised by life and the world often have ambiguous answers, if they have discernible answers at all. The books of Job and Ecclesiastes illustrate this perfectly. In both, very few questions about the difficulties of life, injustice, and purpose are given a clear answer. Instead, when answers are not forthcoming we are instructed to "repent in dust and ashes" in the face of God's might (Job 42:6). The Preacher in Ecclesiastes reminds us over and over, regardless of the virtue or vice being described, that "all is vanity" (Eccl 12:8). While more typical worldview approaches often aim to equip students with preset responses and arm them with proofs, the approach I am advocating aims to develop depth of discernment *despite* the presence of ambiguity in the world. Living well in the world that God has made often requires more than clear answers. To face ambiguity head-on requires imagination.[14]

The cultivation of wisdom through a Christian imagination is one big way Christian educators can prepare students to face an uncertain

---

14. Cf. Beth Green, "Present Tense: Christian Education in Secular Time," in *Innovating Christian Education Research*, ed. Johannes M. Luetz and Beth Green (Singapore: Springer, 2021), 21–22.

world. This means equipping students with breadth of mind, sentiments of sympathy, and depth of understanding of human nature and the human condition. Wisdom with people, wisdom in understanding a sometimes-bewildering world, and wisdom in understanding oneself can be garnered only by deep reflection on a wide variety of human experiences. The picture of reality that the Scriptures paint for us and the response required of us (as in those examples of Job and Ecclesiastes) means that we ought to arm ourselves with wisdom rather than pat answers.

How do we do that? The answer that the Christian West offered for many centuries was to read great books, books that form the imagination toward wisdom. Wisdom doesn't require a great books education or a classical education. But wisdom is certainly helped along by guided reading through the richest works of culture and reflection, works that offer striking insight into the human experience and the human soul. Therefore, the focus on wisdom in my formulation of Christian worldview education requires a focus on the humanities. Christian schools, colleges, and universities ought to offer rich humanities programs in the great books tradition.

What should our students be reading? Great books from Christian authors like Augustine of Hippo, Charles Dickens, Fyodor Dostoyevsky, Thomas Aquinas, John Milton, and Flannery O'Connor. But they should also read the great works of the pre-Christian and non-Christian world, including luminaries like Confucius, Homer, Herodotus, Plato, Aristotle, Cicero, Marx, and Nietzsche. Why read these? Well, on top of the wisdom about the human condition described above, students who engage with the great books are better equipped to become leaders. The greatest leaders of the last five hundred years often enjoyed a rich education in the great books. If Christian institutions want to produce wise leaders who will have an impact on our decaying culture, having a rich humanities program will go a long way. Graduates won't just have answers to worldview questions; they will possess a wisdom that will place them in good stead to make a big impact on their world. Within this Christian worldview framework, Christian institutions are freed up to equip students to be both combatants and ambassadors, good listeners and powerful persuaders, humble and courageous, critical and open, wise and winsome, connected to the past and ready for the future. This can be achieved by aiming at wisdom. The worldview will follow, of course. Setting students up with wisdom, particularly the wisdom of the great books, will have a deep and long impact.

But how can we ensure that our curriculum is truly a Christian one? If we abandon Christian worldview as a normative and deductive concept, what determines what goes in or out of a Christian institution's curriculum? This is an important question for any person or group committed to Christian education and leads to my third prescription. The most common response to the curriculum question is to do what everyone else is doing but add in Bible verses, have devotions in class, and filter content through biblical theological paradigms. But is baptizing secular education enough? A better approach is to educate students in the Christian tradition. This is linked to the second source of wisdom mentioned above, but it is also linked to my prescription for teaching great books. Christian institutions ought to teach not only Christian doctrine, but Christian literature, Christian history, and Christian thought more generally. Christian institutions should not merely be teaching history in a Christian way; they should also be teaching Christian history. Students at Christian schools and colleges should know about the history of the church. They should know about the history of Christian ideas. They should be familiar with the great Christian traditions of poetry, literature, and philosophy. Teach students *who our people are*. Teach them who they can draw on for Christian wisdom. And if they don't embrace Christianity, teach them to recognize Christians with fondness.

The fourth prescription is an administrative one, particularly pertinent for schools, colleges, and universities: we should do away with the requirement to have particular bureaucratic markers of

"Christianness" in our curriculum documentation and syllabi. If, as I am arguing, worldview is not to be understood as deductive, that means worldview is no longer prescriptive. Indeed, the Christian worldview approach to education described in this book essentially means an education pointing students in the direction of wisdom about the world, God, and themselves. It is an education where the Christian distinctives are Christian catechesis and the pursuit of truth and wisdom wherever they might be found. This means we don't need to measure a course of study by the inclusion (or exclusion) of Christian worldview elements. We don't need "Christian world-view" learning outcomes, for instance, because there is no monolithic Christian worldview from which we are deducing the markers of worldview faithfulness. We don't measure teaching performance on the number of Bible verses included in the lesson plan, or on whether they did a devotion at the beginning of class that was linked to the content of the class. Worldview should no longer be viewed as a bureaucratic requirement, nor should the question of being able to teach from a Christian worldview be a problem to be overcome for educators. Worldview is the aim. Worldview is not the means to the end; it *is* the end.

Faithfulness and Education

Where, then, does this leave us in our understanding of Christian education? This proposal might be unsettling for some people, especially those given to seeing Christian faithfulness in education in terms of allegiance to a worldview. Indeed, it raises the question of how we are to reconcile this with the common conception of the Christian educator in evangelical circles. Abraham Kuyper once said to a gathering of Christian school teachers that they had "been used, by the grace of God, to throw up more and more bulwarks against the unholy forces that had already made great progress in taking possession of our people and seizing the heart of the nation."[15] Does Kuyper's vision of

---

15. Abraham Kuyper, "Speech Marking the Fiftieth Anniversary of the Christian Teachers Association," in Abraham Kuyper, *On Education*, ed. Wendy Naylor and Harry Van Dyke

Christian education fit with the understanding of worldview I argue
for in this book? If Christian worldview becomes an end rather than
a means, and the deductive understanding of worldview is no longer
deployed, what happens to "Christian" teaching? What does it mean
to be a faithful Christian teacher, given my conclusions?

In the first place, I want to draw attention to the way this new
framework calls educators to a certain kind of Christian faithfulness.
Teaching wisdom to build a worldview requires something substantial of the teacher that typical worldview education philosophies do
not. It requires excellence and mastery of that which is being taught.
I am not suggesting that we need to severely limit teaching beyond
the ken of our specialist disciplines. I am suggesting that this vision
of Christian education requires something of Christian teachers that
might not be required in the old worldview framework. Your job as
an educator is to invite students to search for truth and thereby grow
in wisdom. This truth points to a vision of reality that results in good
action within that reality. The responsibility here is great. We are finite,
and our minds are affected by the fall. Thankfully, God is gracious.
We can reflect on the world that God has made, and we can understand some of the relations between things in the world such that we
might pass on our limited knowledge to others. Faithfulness looks like
pursuing wisdom as educators, especially in our areas of educational
responsibility, to draw others toward that wisdom.

Faithful Christian teaching doesn't look like using the Bible as
much as possible or teaching from textbooks that claim to be presenting a Christian worldview. Faithful Christian teaching looks like pursuing and teaching the truth wherever it might be found. The French
Reformer John Calvin wrote in his commentary on the Epistle to
Titus, "All truth is from God; and consequently if wicked men have
said anything that is true and just, we ought to not reject it; for it has
come from God. Besides, all things are of God; and, therefore, why

should it not be lawful to dedicate to his glory everything that can properly be employed for such a purpose?"[16]

This is the attitude we all should have toward truth. We are not primarily interested in truth prepackaged with the Christian worldview. As I argued in chapter 2, we need to move on from the combat mindset that originally ignited Christian worldview thinking. We are still in a cosmic war, but the weapons we fight with in Christian education need to change because they aren't fit for purpose. Faithfulness in education doesn't look like intellectual combat through the pitting of the Christian worldview against other worldviews. Worldview talk needs to change from means to ends. Christian worldviews are the aim, and to get there we teach wisdom by pointing to truth. Therefore, faithful Christian teaching in all disciplines is the imparting of wisdom through the seeking of truth.

I want to drill a little further down here by reflecting on something Nicholas Wolterstorff once said about Christian learning and the differentiation between Christians and non-Christians. He said, "The aim of Christian learning is *not* to be different or distinctive but to be *faithful*."[17] This seems to be a call to do away with the idea of Christian *intellectual* distinctives. But we know that Wolterstorff affirms that there is a substantive difference between the scholarship of believers and that of non-believers, so it can't be that. Rather, he wants us to stop using difference in the results of teaching and intellectual inquiry as a badge of honor or a marker of faithfulness. In my opinion, it is quite natural that Christians would call on different sources in their teaching and learning, and I have argued above to that end. Wolterstorff suggests as much, too.[18]

---

16. John Calvin, Commentary on Titus 1:12; John Calvin, *Commentaries on the Epistles to Timothy, Titus, and Philemon*, trans. William Pringle (Grand Rapids: Eerdmans, 1959), 300–301.

17. Nicholas Wolterstorff, "A Case for Disinterested Learning," in *Educating for Shalom: Essays in Christian Higher Education*, ed. Clarence W. Joldersma and Gloria Goris Stronks (Grand Rapids: Eerdmans, 2004), 106.

18. Wolterstorff, "Case for Disinterested Learning," 107.

But how should we measure this faithfulness? Given everything argued above, we need not be interested in faithfulness to a particular intellectual framework that we might label a "Christian worldview." Rather, we should be seeking faithfulness to the message of the gospel of Christ. One obvious way that a Christian teacher could fail at faithfulness to the gospel would be to deny it or bring it into serious doubt. Therefore, doctrine must be one of the measures of faithfulness, demonstrated by adherence to the creeds and confessions of the church. But aside from creedal fidelity (including to something like an institutional statement of faith), the way that Christian teaching and learning works itself out is surely too subtle to call for prescriptive intellectual markers and results. The Christian gospel affects the whole person, and Christian teaching ought to be a result of the transformation wrought by the Spirit on a believer. The real faithfulness we should be looking for is God's rather than our own. Both kinds of faithfulness matter, but the former has more impact on Christian educators.

Reframing distinctive Christian education around faithfulness means the way we think about distinctives in Christian education will change. There will be distinctives, but they will organically emerge as teachers and students expose themselves to the best Christian and non-Christian sources and the best Christian and secular thinking, while having the Holy Spirit work with them in the education process. This approach to faithfulness points to the need for Christian educators to grow an affinity with the intellectual and spiritual traditions of the Christian faith. In cultures that are marked by widespread unbelief, the distinctives of Christian institutions will appear quite naturally if this is pursued. Faithfulness will also be evidenced by excellence. The humble pursuit of knowledge and truth, informed by the Scriptures and the Christian intellectual tradition, will help students attain a Christian worldview. This book doesn't cover the complex question of pedagogy, but assuming an effective pedagogy, this approach to the intellectual aspect of teaching and learning will bear the fruit of faithfulness. Faithful Christian teaching ought to be marked less by the distinctive outcomes and more by the way it is carried out.

Conclusion

When you gaze upon the mosaic of the Mausoleum of Galla Placidia, you are not being asked to make an intellectual account of the symbolism or provide a rational critique of the inaccurate scale of the aspects of the mosaic. Rather, you are being called to cry out in your spirit to the God who governs the entire cosmos. While it does not proscribe it, the vision of reality portrayed in the mausoleum is not promoting rational reflection. Rather, it prompts doxology. Like the apostle Paul at the end of Romans 11, worshipers are moved to cry out to God. "Oh, the depth of the riches and wisdom and knowledge of God! How unsearchable are his judgments and how inscrutable his ways!" (Rom 11:33). We cry out in praise and wonder to the mighty God who ordered all things, who upholds all things, and who governs all things. When we grasp reality, even if that grasp is incomplete and limited, we are still moved to offer a sacrifice of praise and thanksgiving in response to what we understand.

A Christian worldview education ought to have a similar result. But it is worth recalling that the worldview education described here is not working from a completed mosaic. A Christian education ought to be focused on wisdom, on the laying of tiles of wisdom in the mosaic. When we see the mosaic, even in an incomplete fashion, both student and teacher will be moved by the majesty and magnificence of the cosmic reality present there. A Christian education ought to be one that invites doxology from the students. Note that doxology is a response to what God has done or said. The learning should prompt praise. Truth is truth, wherever it is found. This means that we don't need to make truth godly or Christian. All truth is of God, says Calvin, whether it comes from the mouth of a Christian or a pagan. It is the response to this truth that matters.

The French philosopher Simone Weil wrote on the links between education and religious piety in her essay "Reflections on the Right

Use of School Studies with a View to the Love of God." The general thrust of this essay is that study requires "attention" to the thing being studied. School studies have, according to Weil, a sacramental quality to them in that they point us to Jesus Christ through the attitude and habit of attention, but also in the pointed pursuit of truth for its own sake. This attention directs the learner toward "a little fragment of particular truth," which is a "pure image of the unique, eternal, and living Truth."[19] There are, then, doxological and intellectual aspects of the Christian response to truth.

The study of God's world, God himself, and ourselves will spur us on to truth, which in turn points us to Truth. He who is the Truth is the ultimate aim of our teaching and our learning. The habit of attention to the small and the narrow can lead students to consider the higher truths. Indeed, it ought to. The inculcation and application of wisdom will lead to prudent living and knowledge of reality, to be sure. But ultimately it can lead to the student proclaiming the greatness of our King, who rules over all. A Christian education understood as a mosaic building project is a lot like Weil's argument for the study of small-t truth leading to the contemplation of Truth himself.

A Christian education that is faithful in the pursuit and imparting of wisdom is the best kind of worldview education. Students will receive the wisdom of the Scriptures, the wisdom of the Christian tradition, and the wisdom of the ages. In doing so, they will be equipped to reach for reality in a way that will point them to the maker of that reality. In pursuing wisdom, they will encounter the Wisdom of God, and in pursuing truth they will meet the Truth. This is Christian education. It is not prepackaged answers or artificial theological frameworks. It is the seeking of wisdom in the world, in the Scriptures, and in the Christian tradition. The pursuit of a Christian worldview, in this sense, is the pursuit of a vision of reality that prompts doxology and worship. Is this not why we educate?

---

19. Simone Weil, "Reflections on the Right Use of School Studies with a View to the Love of God," in *The Great Tradition: Classic Readings on What It Means to Be an Educated Human Being*, ed. Richard M. Gamble (Washington, DC: ISI, 2007), 589–92.

Chapter 6

Conclusion:
Wisdom *and* Worldview

No one is quite sure why the Mausoleum of Galla Placidia was built. It is obviously a place of Christian worship. However, the precise intended function of the chapel is lost to history. Yet the intention of the ceiling mosaic is clear. Its purpose was to provide those who enter the chapel with a vision of reality designed to captivate the senses and move people to doxological worship. The mosaics were placed piece-by-piece by numerous craftsmen, most of whom did not have the privilege of understanding the entire design of the mosaics. Rather, the master craftsman, the chief mosaicist, possessed the all-important overall design in his head and on parchment. This mosaicist knew what vision of cosmic reality needed to be presented on the ceiling, whether by his own design or at the behest of his patron. The worshiper is confronted by imagery that forces her to contemplate the magnificence of the Christian vision of the cosmos and the glory of the creator.

This mosaic imagery is the one I have woven throughout the book to guide our reconsideration of worldview as an educational framework. The Christian worldview concept, as it currently stands in the Christian world, doesn't work. In chapters 1 and 2, I explained why. Worldview's historical provenance shows that we are wielding it in ways that are not suited to the concept or our context. Worldview language was originally used by Christian thinkers in cultural and religious combat, at a time of heightened intellectual conflict in Europe. We are not in that kind of situation anymore. Worldview discourse made some sense in a liberal and pluralistic public square, but our approach to speaking in public needs to adapt to a world where Christianity is neither respected nor understood.[1] As part of a broader shift in cultural engagement, Christian educators should move from defending ground to taking ground by adopting a new posture in our education philosophy. As I argue in later chapters, we should move from deductive worldview thinking to a inductive approach, which should be a part of adapting to a changing culture. Appealing to Christian worldview also doesn't work philosophically or theologically because the concept is so vague as to be indefensible. Both factors make worldview a blunt instrument in educational settings. Worldview began to be used in Christian institutions in the early twentieth century as a way of defining Christian education. However, it is not a helpful or adequate tool in this regard. Should we replace it? I don't believe so. Rather, we need to rethink it.

To this end, I have suggested that we ought to understand the attaining of a worldview as an inductive process, much like the construction of a mosaic. Where it differs from mosaic construction is in the overall understanding of the big picture (that is, the Christian worldview). Previously, Christian worldview thinking tended toward a totalizing and triumphalist assessment of the ability of mere mortals to see reality properly. We need to temper this significantly. We need to understand that we are limited, sometimes in the extreme. We can know about reality because reality is stable, orderly, and accessible. Knowledge of reality is also something that we can acquire little by little. I argued for this in chapter 3 in my presentation of the Christian realism of Herman Bavinck. As creatures and learners, we can know

---

1. For more on this, see my "Three Worlds and Two Christianities," *Mere Orthodoxy*, January 11, 2023, https://mereorthodoxy.com/three-worlds-and-two-christianities.

the mind of God in his creation, but we can do so in only a limited way. Education is the gradual building up of knowledge about reality. Rather than learning high-level principles and then deducing how aspects of knowledge about reality fit into them, the acquisition of knowledge is an inductive process. Therefore, education is largely by induction. It is like laying one *tessera* at a time on a mosaic.

But what is the content of this inductive education? What are the tiles of the worldview mosaic? Chapter 4 answered this question: wisdom. A Christian worldview education lays wisdom tiles on the worldview mosaic. Education is the presentation, imparting, and pursuit of wisdom. In the context of a Christian education, this wisdom comes in two forms. A Christian education will impart practical wisdom: wisdom about God's world and wisdom about human beings. Students with practical wisdom will be equipped to act in a way that fits with the order of created reality. A Christian education will also impart spiritual wisdom, a wisdom that inclines the heart of the student to pursue communion with the Wisdom of God in Jesus Christ. Students equipped with spiritual wisdom will know how to know God (even if they do not yet). When we help students access the wisdom that is embedded in creation and revelation, we help them place their tiles on the worldview mosaic.

But do we need to retain the term "Christian worldview" when it seems that all we are talking about now is wisdom? In chapter 5, I argued that students who are taught wisdom have been given a vision of reality. That vision of reality is necessarily limited rather than complete and all-encompassing, but it frames all life and action within a larger vision of existence, a vision that prompts students (and educators) to worship and praise. This is still a Christian education, after all. Our aim is still the glory and praise of the Triune God. In that context, I argued that Christian faithfulness as educators looks different if we adhere to this new understanding of worldview. Faithfulness looks like excellence, but it also looks like a careful use of the sources that God has given us in the world, in the church, and in the Scriptures.

What should we do now, especially if we are in Christian institutions where worldview language frames our mission and curriculum? Pastors and parents might reconsider the use of worldview frameworks in parenting and discipleship contexts. But whatever your situation, I do not intend this book to be a distraction or a hindrance. My core claim here has been that the old idea of Christian worldview needs to be reimagined. None of us has access to a complete Christian worldview. Therefore, the Christian worldview is not the starting point for framing Christian education. Instead, we should think of education as the process of acquiring spiritual and practical wisdom. This process is akin to the building of a work of art. Christian education is the construction of a worldview that reflects created reality and informs wise action in light of that reality. Rather than being the *framework* for a Christian education, Christian worldview is the *goal* of education.

Seven Theses on Christian Worldview

Thesis 1: The current Christian worldview concept doesn't work. We need to rethink it.

Thesis 2: Reality is stable and knowable, and therefore we can learn about it piece by piece.

Thesis 3: Education is the science of relations, where students join with educators in learning about the relationship of themselves to creation, to God, and the relations between everything else.

Thesis 4: The content of a Christian worldview education is wisdom, both practical and spiritual.

Thesis 5: A Christian worldview is gained by induction. We attain a Christian worldview by growing in rightly apprehending created reality through the gaining of wisdom.

Thesis 6: Wisdom is available to everyone through three main sources, apart from nature itself: the Bible, the Christian tradition, and the world. These are the sources available to Christian educators.

Thesis 7: Christian worldview education is the construction of worldviews by the teaching of wisdom.

Theses Explained

1. *The current Christian worldview concept doesn't work. We need to rethink it.*

The concept of "Christian Worldview" arose in an age of Christian pluralism. Beginning with James Orr and Abraham Kuyper in the late nineteenth century, worldview thinking was adapted to fit the polemical context that the church found itself in as Western culture shifted away from Christianity. Christian worldview education emerged in the latter part of the twentieth century as a defensive weapon in an age of cultural combat. Our situation is different now and requires a different approach to worldview in education.

2. *Reality is stable and knowable, and therefore we can learn about it piece by piece.*

Christian educators ought to embrace the epistemology of Christian realism, which affirms the existence of objective, created reality that generally corresponds with our sense perception of it.

3. *Education is the science of relations, where students join with educators in learning about the relationship of themselves to creation, to God, and the relations between everything else.*

As educators and students, we are reaching for a particular vision of reality that we know exists and that we see glimpses of. Yet our experience doesn't give us the master plan. Indeed, our apprehension of that plan is extremely limited. We need sense experience to construct an understanding of reality, one that we believe corresponds (however imperfectly) with the overarching, meaningful design of that reality. We expand and refine our understanding of reality through learning. Education is the process whereby we develop relations between the learner and the world, between the learner and God. In doing this, the learner will also grasp the relations between those different parts of reality outside of the learner.

4. The content of a Christian worldview education is wisdom, both practical and spiritual.

Christian worldview education can be understood not as an attempt to perfect someone's understanding but as the process of helping students think and act in accordance with the wisdom of God. In gaining practical wisdom, students learn how to understand the world and reality through the gaining of knowledge and skills that will help them live a wise, fruitful life in the creation of God. Spiritual wisdom cannot be gained in the same way that we gain practical wisdom, because this wisdom is connected to saving faith. The integration of true faith with practical wisdom is much more a task for the learner than the teacher. Nevertheless, Christian educators should be purveyors of spiritual wisdom, aiming to make students wise unto salvation.

5. A Christian worldview is gained by induction. We attain a Christian worldview by growing in rightly apprehending created reality through the gaining of wisdom.

People gain a Christian worldview by growing in wisdom, which gives them a true picture of reality. While high-level principles are important, learning typically takes place gradually, and the refining of our grasp of God's creation and our relation to it and to him requires time and effort. One major way the Scriptures image this process is the person growing in wisdom. Therefore, a Christian worldview, which is evidenced when someone rightly apprehending themselves and their relation to God and his world is attained through growth in wisdom.

6. Wisdom is available to everyone through three main sources, apart from nature itself: the Bible, the Christian tradition, and the world. These are the sources available to Christian educators.

A Christian education that is faithful in the pursuit of, and imparting of, wisdom is a true worldview education. In this kind of education, people will access the wisdom of the Scriptures, the wisdom of the Christian tradition, and the wisdom of the ages. Each of these sources holds promise for a Christian worldview education, because God's truth can be found in a variety of places and ascertained by a variety of people. Christian educators should use these sources of wisdom.

7. Christian worldview education is the construction of worldviews by the teaching of wisdom.

A true Christian worldview education is like the construction of a work of art. Students and disciples join with educators in building up their worldview through the gathering of, and synthesis of, wisdom. This wisdom-shaped apprehension of reality will point them to the maker of that reality. In pursuing wisdom, they will encounter the Wisdom of God, and in pursuing truth they will meet the Truth. This is the highest goal of Christian worldview education.

Acknowledgments

It was an honor to receive a research grant from the Australian Research Theology Foundation so I could dedicate more time to completing this book. The grant allowed me to think and write more than I otherwise would have across late 2021 and early 2022. I'm also grateful to my colleagues at Christian Heritage College (CHC) for providing me with resources of time and space during this period. CHC was a fertile institutional base to work on these ideas, as I was constantly surrounded by people dedicated to the cause of distinctively Christian education.

Editors are pedagogues. I learned how to turn this manuscript into a book through the guidance and encouragement of Todd Hains and Elliot Ritzema. Todd took my idea and applied his enthusiasm and wisdom. Elliot allowed me to gloat about Budapest coffee houses. More importantly, he found what was wanting in the manuscript's details and argument. John Barach both copyedited and interrogated the manuscript, making it a better book. I am in your debt. I'm also grateful for the generosity of the wider Lexham Press team and feel blessed to publish with a press that cares about the quality and faithfulness of the content and the physical product. *Quod bonum Dei quidem donum est* (Augustine of Hippo, *De civitate Dei*, XV.22).

The ideas in this book were given early exposure in several venues. These contexts included the Transforming Vision Conference at CHC in March 2021, and the Transformed conference jointly hosted by Reformed Theological College and Christian Education National in May 2021. I was also privileged to present a keynote at the Associated Christian Schools teachers' conference in July 2021, and further trialed my ideas in a presentation to the Christian Studies department at Redlands College in the same year. Chapter 2 was presented at two conferences, one jointly hosted by Australian Catholic University, Deakin University, and the Religious History Association in July 2021, and the other at the Australian Christian Higher Education Association Conference in September 2021. The substance of this chapter was published in *Church History* and appears here with the gracious permission of the editors of that journal.

I have benefitted immensely from the wisdom of colleagues and friends. Craig Murison and Ben Myers provided invaluable input into my thinking across the drafting process. Joel Hughes was a consistent interlocutor and friend, an excellent combination if there ever was one. He offered me a regular diet of discussion and brought an invaluable perspective as I was writing. Johannes Solymosi was another friend and critic who helped me navigate some of the treacherous waters of Christian worldview as it relates to schools. Ben, Joel, and Johannes each read the manuscript in draft form and offered invaluable feedback that improved the book immensely. Thanks go to each of you for carving out the time to dedicate to this task. Bruce Pass also supplied me with friendship, Bavinck expertise, and feedback on key sections of an early draft.

I also want to acknowledge Jonathan Staggs, Bill Berends, Chris Prior, Mike Thompson, and Ben Saunders, who all offered encouragement and input at various points. Thanks to Lucila Feldman for pointing me to prescient sections in the works of Charlotte Mason and stimulating my thinking on key aspects of my argument. My appreciation also extends to Stephen Morton and the CHC Library staff, as well as the University of Queensland Library. These fine institutions supplied me with a variety of resources across the project.

To my families—I am grateful to my spiritual family at Shore Hope Presbyterian Church for praying, serving, and supporting this project in seen and unseen ways. To my father and mother, Paul and Meredith: my love and thanks will never properly repay what you have given me, which included a Christian home and a Christian education.

Finally, to my *oikos*—my children, Lydia, Lesla, Judson, Adelaide, and Calvin are all inspirations for this book. I am invested in the question of Christian education more than ever because God has gifted me with real people to nurture. I love you all fiercely. Last and certainly not least, my wife, Hayley, has gone above and beyond in supporting the work needed to complete this book. Her constant care, interest, and intellectual engagement in the big questions I have sought to address here were all acts of love. This book is for you, my love.

Victoria Point, Queensland
February 2024

Subject and Author Index

and reason, 80
and redemption, 83, 84
spiritual, 85, 86, 87–88
as a totality concept, 80
and worldview, 72, 74, 94
Wolters, Albert, 5
Wolterstorff, Nicholas, 6, 11, 116
worldview
  analysis, 12, 14–15
  and culture, 13
  Christian, 10
  combat concept, 13, 30, 31, 39
  criticism, 3, 5, 7, 8–15

deductive, 17, 21, 47, 55, 95, 99
definition, 4, 15
education, sources for, 106–9, 115
higher education, 9
history of, 2, 25–41
inductive versus deductive, 47, 64, 101
intellectual, 5
questions, 12
requirements, 113–14
and teaching, 97, 117
and wisdom, 72, 74, 94
Wright, N. T., 12

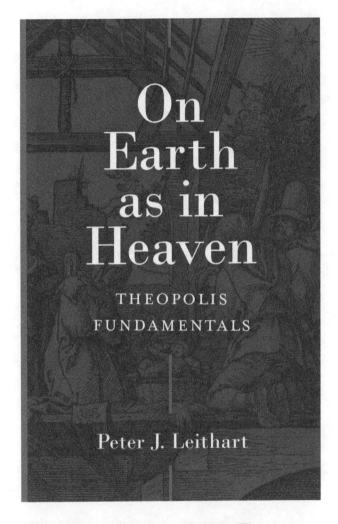

On
Earth
as in
Heaven

THEOPOLIS
FUNDAMENTALS

Peter J. Leithart

ALSO AVAILABLE
FROM LEXHAM PRESS

Explore how the heavenly city of God resurrects
the cities of men in *On Earth as in Heaven*.